Uncommon
COMMON WOMEN

Errata

Photos nine, ten, and eleven should be credited as follows:

9.   Homestead of an African American family near Gutherie, Oklahoma Territory, 1889.   Swearingen Collection. Courtesy of the Western History Collections, University of Oklahoma Library, Norman, Oklahoma.

10. A gathering of Native Americans in Indian Territory, possibly including descendants of African Americans. Hudson Collection. Courtesy of the Western History Collections, University of Oklahoma Library, Norman, Oklahoma.

11. Page of sheet music. "Before I'd Be a Slave."

Uncommon
COMMON WOMEN

***

Ordinary Lives of
the West

***

Anne M. Butler

***

Ona Siporin

UTAH STATE UNIVERSITY PRESS

Logan, Utah

To Our Mothers

Jean Atkins Posey
—Anne

Coral White
—Ona

Utah State University Press
Logan, Utah 84322-7800

Typography by WolfPack

Library of Congress Cataloging-in-Publication Data
Butler, Anne M., 1938-
  Uncommon common women / Anne M. Butler, Ona Siporin.
    p. cm.
  Includes bibliographical references and index.
  ISBN 0-87421-209-X. — ISBN 0-87421-210-3 (pbk.)
  1. Women—West (U.S.)—History. I. Siporin, Ona. II. Title.
HQ1438.W45B87 1996
305.4'0978—dc

                                                        2096-10025
                                                        CIP

Contents

Acknowledgments

The Utah State University Special Collections and Archives division of the Merrill Library assisted us in accumulating our illustrations. Surveyor of Pictures, Peter F. Schmid, expended his considerable talents and much time in helping us identify the appropriate choices for this volume. The trove of materials he placed before us made our own university a valuable resource. As a result, many of the photographs that document our text have been drawn from Utah State University. We direct a warm thank you to Milton T. Theall of Weston, Massachusetts, who generously made available the frontier photograph album of his parents, Delbert and Charlotte Theall. Glenda Riley contributed excellent selections from her private collection. Nelson B. Wadsworth of Logan, Utah, aided us in the preparation of all the photographs and taught us much about preservation of the images of the past.

Any project comes to fruition because of the combined efforts of many persons. We express our gratitude to each, but we retain sole responsibility for any flaws in our publication. We give a special nod to Susan Switzer and Joan Fincutter of the Girl Scouts of America for getting us started. At the *Western Historical Quarterly*, we thank our senior editor, Clyde A. Milner II, who so thoroughly endorses the intellectual endeavors of his staff with verbal encouragement and practical advice. In that same office, we thank Barbara Stewart, who listened to our endless discussions and singlehandedly spread the word about *Uncommon Common Women* through Utah. Graduate students Steve Amerman and Jim Feldman worked without complaint on slide preparation, attended our presentations, and sustained us with an unending supply of good cheer and laughter.

It was an honor to be sponsored by the Utah Humanities Council from 1994-1996. Our association with the council, especially Alex Page, allowed us the opportunity to participate in this important cultural initiative. We thank the many communities of Utah citizens who greeted us with kindness and attention.

Special thanks to Lana Johnson and Glenda Riley, both of whom helped us take the program beyond the local level and introduced us to our national audience.

Our association with the staff of the Utah State University Press has been most cordial. We reserve our deepest professional thanks and respect for press director Michael Spooner for making this book possible.

My children, Dan Porterfield and Kate Porterfield, enhance all that I do with their constant interest, love, and good humor. As for my husband, Jay—he drove to presentations in every kind of foul weather, dragged equipment, showed hundreds of slides, and gave important critiques. He brought to *Uncommon Common Women*, as he does everything in my life, great joy and fun.

Anne M. Butler

Lee Austin of KUSU-FM was the first to publicly support my work with western stories, and I thank him for introducing me to the joys of radio production and for encouraging me. Several of these stories have been edited by Jared Farmer. His incisive sense of language has saved me from much embarrassment. Finally, my family is an unfailing source of encouragement, humor, patience, and spiritual and intellectual challenge. They bear me with them.

Ona Siporin

Preface

A NOTE ON HISTORY

Historians love the past. They delve into it with a passion that bemuses the non-practitioner. The world expects this of historians—that they should be the keepers of the sacred events and great leaders of other eras. From among vast collections of documents and photographs, maps and artifacts, scholars piece together the patterns of earlier societies and the people who lived in them. They pore over military strategies, tariff lists, and election returns to explain how one nation thrived as another declined, why one army triumphed as another collapsed. If the general population evinces only mild interest in the details of these endeavors, it remains assured that our formal historical legacy is carefully preserved.

Yet, while the world was not watching, historians altered the boundaries of their professional love to encompass a much broader and more vibrant definition of history. Historians have expanded the scope of their scholarship beyond the arena of yesterday's governments and public figures to a more inclusive worldview that considers the impact of lesser-known people in the emergence of a society's heritage. Women, children, ethnic groups, minority cultures, everyday life, the nameless and the faceless—these constitute the lively new ingredients in historical research. Not only have these themes gained currency among scholars, but they have attracted the interest of all manner of citizens, who finally seem to understand that history need not be the exclusive province of academicians.

The result has been an explosion of publication that not only peels back the layers of our nation's history, revealing rich new textures, but stimulates discussion among scholars and non-scholars alike. It is this latter group that has so energized history within communities and cultures. Awakened to the connection between ordinary folk as historical players and the experiences of their own families, Americans now demonstrate a new zest for knowledge of the common people who built our cities, our towns, our regions, and our nation. As never before, they see that America's heritage embraces their own kin and clan.

The history accounts in this volume seek to address that personal interest, especially in relation to western women. Herein are short pieces, accounts of some women who lived in a region that by the early twentieth century appeared to define a peculiar element in the American character. Scholars may want more original research; non-scholars may wish for more examples. Both must turn elsewhere. This history is intended only to suggest, for a general audience, some of the ways in which ordinary women, of diverse cultures and ethnic backgrounds, gave voice to their lives in the American West. In this book, the history makes one thread, the stories a second, the photographs a third; together they weave a fabric of women's lives.

Anne M. Butler

A NOTE ON STORIES

he stories, or sketches, in this book were created to be told aloud to a live audience. In the shapes of ink you see here on the page, the narratives become static, a state unnatural to them. Though symbols are handy, they are not language itself and they cannot do what the living, spoken language can. Given this, it is important to remember that you are reading only one version of the many each of these stories can be. In oral performance, the story is ever new, revealing in its singularity something about the lives and characters of these women that has never before been revealed.

So I ask you not to rely too much on first impressions. Consider these pieces only an introduction to Little Joe, Manuela, Catherine Wetherill, Fruma, and the others. In another telling these fine women would reveal different aspects of their lives and thoughts. Like anyone, each of these women is a paradox: always the same, but always different. The more I know them—and I have known some longer than others—the more extraordinary each of them becomes. Like any person, each of these women contains a universe, the beauties and secrets of which are discernible only by listening countless times to her story. I am honored to be part of this community, and hope you will enjoy meeting these women.

People ask me where I find my stories. I find them everywhere I turn, but speaking only of the stories in this book, I have three main sources: archives, general written material, and oral informants.

The majority of the stories herein are based on historical figures; some are based on historical phenomena. "Fruma was my children's great-grandmother. Manuela truly was incarcerated in a men's prison. Ynes Mexia was a noted botanist. Catherine Wetherill is not to my knowledge a historical figure, but I have found in archives and heard from oral sources of children thought to have died, who were buried under rocks—later to be discovered alive. And, in truth, some babies were "buried" in trees.

There is a list of sources at the end of this book for those interested in more detail.

Ona Siporin

Introduction

We never expected to spend so much time with these uncommon common women. They came into our lives, near Bismarck, North Dakota, as a presentation for the Girl Scouts of America. That occasion, in 1991, introduced us to the concept of melding history with storytelling to fashion a performance about the lives of western women. We were as delighted by the experience of working together as we were by the warm reception we received from the Girl Scouts, though treading into the area of joint performance marked uncharted waters.

After our trip to North Dakota, flushed with the fun of our shared efforts, we decided to build on our ideas about the ordinary women who deserve attention for their western experience. We took our original presentation and added, deleted, reshaped, rethought. Within a short time, we found we had a performance that shifted and changed as we worked with it and as we became closer friends. Thus came into being the program we called *Uncommon Common Women.*

With an endorsement from the Utah Humanities Council and the power of word of mouth, *Uncommon Common Women* started to circulate through the Beehive State. We received invitations from women's groups, church organizations, historical societies, civic agencies, and individuals. We visited small towns, universities, and national and state forest campgrounds. In all of these places, audiences overwhelmed us with their enthusiastic response to this marriage of two mediums. Most especially, women, young and old, spoke about how *Uncommon Common Women* touched their memories and their hearts.

The joy of companionship, the intellectual pleasure of the performances, the warm reactions of listeners—these alone sustained us. Yet, time and again, people asked about our plans to publish a book. We deflected these inquiries with a laugh. It was enough to have bonded two such different styles.

We had not counted on the persuasive powers of Michael Spooner, director of the Utah State University Press. Through his vision, we came to see the potential for this book. He developed the practical approach to *Uncommon Common Women* as a literary presentation. We acknowledge our intellectual debt to him and thank him for adding another dimension to our work.

Nonetheless, each of us brought some fears to this project, because in it we have stepped aside from our usual categories of professional expertise. We worried about how the vibrancy of the storyteller, working with a live audience, would translate to the written word, and how the formality of the research scholar could be converted to historical vignettes.

In part, we solved this dilemma by centering our individual goals on a common word—"story." As our oral presentation evolved over time, we came to recognize that our separate senses of narrative ultimately provided the unifying element in *Uncommon Common Women.*

For the historian, the word "story"—as imaginative construction—often symbolizes that which should be discarded or stripped away from the pursuit of history. Historians relentlessly seek to cast off the fictions that shroud historical characters in layers of inaccuracy and cloud the patterns of history. Scholars use primary documents, research, and analysis as their weapons for battling popular misconceptions about people and time periods. They want to look at history through a wide lens, one that reveals diversity of experience, thus illuminating some portion of historical truth.

For the teller, research and primary documents act as a catalyst. They inform imagination, instruct diction, and propel voice. The teller focuses on incident and detail, rather than broad statement—listening for the spirit of a person or a people and creating a situation to echo that spirit with integrity. In a weathered hand, a moment of grief, or a conversation, a narrator hopes to elicit an instance of lived experience.

Rather than rejecting each other's approach, we intertwined the two to give a foundation to *Uncommon Common Women.* Our recognition of each other's personal sense of history guides our spoken performance. It is our intention that the pages of this book reflect these dual perceptions in a meaningful way for readers.

The result of our collaboration is this slim volume. Our vision is of a book of little-known women, women of whom general readers will have no knowledge. Our statement is that many women—whether or not they became famous—were persons of courage, of wit, of skill. We do not wish to ignore the better known women of the West, such as Calamity Jane and Belle Starr, but they have been treated at length in other works; it is not our purpose to duplicate those. We look on this book as only one form of our public and private conversations about women over the past several years. We perceive of the parts of this work—fiction, history, photographs—as equally illuminative of women's lives of the latter half of the nineteenth century. That is, we do not consider the history the "real stuff" and the stories and photos merely entertainment. Rather, we are using three approaches to get at lived experience, each approach as true, in its way, as the others: fiction as valid as history and photos, history as valid as fiction and photos, photos as valid as history and fiction. We encourage readers to understand that we attach no hierarchy to genre and that, in our perception, for this book, illustration, history, and fiction function together to make the whole.

This work merely touches women's western lives, in history, tale, and photo. It contains the brief overview, the short story. It leaves much of the woman's world for the reader to explore. The content is merely suggestive, intended to infuse the reader with a desire to learn more about western women. We want only to lure our audiences toward a larger and deeper knowledge of western women, to a perception of some of the race, class, and gender forces that shaped their lives. Although we center on women of the American West in the latter half of the nineteenth century, we are convinced that their essence, in story and in life, transcends the boundaries of region and, in some aspects, of time, to encompass the nature of womanhood.

1

Women of the Prairies

When W. H. D. Koerner's "Madonna of the Prairie" first appeared in 1922, it represented a nostalgia grounded in the American imagination, rather than the realities of nineteenth century pioneer life. The gentle, yet determined features of a young woman, whose Conestoga wagon framed her serenity with a canvas halo, captured what many Americans believed of women who made the long overland trek to unknown western regions. This pioneer image offered a comforting national memory for those who think of women only as "gentle tamers," or stoic, long-suffering "civilizers." For the many Americans who trace their ancestors to the overland migration and point to maternal ancestors by name, these images of courageous pioneer women offer both personal and national visions of courage. The stories of these true-to-life American women run through the whole fabric of the western epic, giving it powerful legitimacy. Yet, along with them run the threads of fiction producing, as in all such historical misconceptions, a saga enveloped by both fact and fancy.

The qualities of endless patience, quiet suffering, and limitless sacrifice appealed to W. H. D. Koerner, who felt keenly about the "loss of the frontier" and its values for American families. Koerner, who painted his western images from his studio in New Jersey, should hardly be castigated, for he clearly embodied the spirit of so many Americans of his time.

That spirit underscores a tale of the West that highlights the settlement experiences of white families and glorifies their struggles

at the expense of other western residents. It is depicted in another
Koerner painting, "The Homesteaders," where bone-weary, yet
refreshingly clean and scrubbed, young farm parents gaze lovingly
on the infant who literally will reap the benefits of their toil.
While the venture of white settlers to populate the West is a rich
and interesting one, in its telling, Americans have often overlooked other groups of people who help to account for the com-
plexity of regional diversity.

An arbitrarily defined geographic area, even one as intriguing
as the West, with its varied terrains and mercurial climate, does
not give home to a single people or culture. Rather, the American
West, with its vast spaces, sweeping vistas, and scrub pines
embraces far more than a few stereotypical weather conditions or
human characters.

For example, white women, as historical entities, lose their
forcefulness, if when accepted at face value, the individual com-
plexities of women's lives are diluted for the sake of a conve-
nient, unchallenging tale. We need only peel back a few layers of
our national misconception to find that western women encountered, challenged, and surmounted a kaleidoscope of experiences. Their stories, individually and collectively, show that in
the West the lives of women assumed myriad shapes.

In the first instance, western women need to be granted a bit
more physical authenticity. The very nature of overland travel
precluded the likelihood of the sanitized "Madonna" in Koerner's
painting. The well-worn clothes, the few items for personal
hygiene, the limits of diet, the demands of pregnancy and childbirth, the daily chores, the rigors of the trek, the uncertainty of
the road ahead—all combined to produce a far more weathered
collection of women than Koerner suggested. If their photographs
are scanned for less of the romance and more of the humanity,
pioneer women radiate a far different kind of beauty. Theirs is a
beauty forged from the reality of life's constant and often searing
experiences.

America's women—native born and immigrant—who became
the overland pioneers, from whose portraits shine solemn eyes of
painful knowledge, earned those haunting expressions. Their

travels changed their lives in ways they had never anticipated before they became pilgrims to the West. Each day brought a different set of events, all shaped by a swirl of forces.

At the very least, on a daily basis, women travelers engaged the many moods of weather, from its most scorching to its most frigid. In shifting furies, the elements went from torrents of rain to throat-parching aridity to torrents of snow. Wind buffeted migrants. Sun baked them. Night froze them. Weather lacked the gentle touch, and it refused containment. It swept across plain and prairie, down gulch and through canyon—and always it careened over great spaces that offered no comfort, little shelter, few places to hide.

Women migrants also encountered a changing cast of characters. Fellow travelers, ethnic groups, Native Americans, religious missionaries, established settlers—all brought a mix of interpersonal exchanges. Some exchanges meant new friendships, broadened horizons. Others resulted in clashes, either verbal or physical. All meant that the human perceptions of women changed because of their western experience.

In this arena of mountain and desert, this maelstrom of heat and cold, this tangle of humanity, modern enthusiasts of the West

need to listen more carefully to the words of women pioneers. They fit no mold; they defied the stereotypes we have thrust upon them. Their voices arose, not as a chorus of platitudes about life, but as the blending of complex harmonies. Theirs was a glorious symphony of women that reverberated off canyon walls and rippled through clear rivers. Boldness, confidence, despair, strength, merriment, courage, sorrow, weariness—all possible expressions of human feeling and experience marked their song. Some trumpeted their womanhood with good spirit; others sounded the occasional discordant note. All contributed to a baroque piece that resonated with individuality.

*O*n the trail and off people found their ways of dying.

Rachel Street was struck by lightning on the open prairie. She saw the storm coming and, mesmerized by its beauty, made no attempt to take cover.

Fourteen-year-old Sarah Coe, wasted and dehydrated from diarrhea, died in her mother's arms in the back of their wagon.

Katherine Hanks, a prostitute, was beaten to death in her shack, her crib, by a jealous patron.

Betsy Rogers, two years old, was kicked in the head by one of the horses. It was his only team, but in the fury of his grief, her father shot the horse.

Anne Judson's friend said she knew a plant that would cure Anne's sore joints—that ached in the humid heat of the Independence summer. The Joe-Pye weed she said. But she didn't know sweet Joe-Pye from white snakeroot, and Anne Judson died of milk sickness.

Samantha Frazer died from a ruptured appendix on a warm spring afternoon on the bank of the Platte River.

On her way to the spring for water, in central Nebraska, Jemima Palmer was suprised by two Cheyenne, who stepped onto the trail from behind a cottonwood. She died on the spot, from terror, though they had only wanted to ask for food.

Anna Erickson, ten years old, was consumed with her brothers and sisters in a field of flame, a prairie fire in central Iowa. They had been picnicking along a stream, when suddenly the rise above them blossomed in hot orange and yellow.

Some say there was a grave every twenty yards along the Oregon Trail.

THE SOD HOUSE

*O*ther pioneer women of the 1850s and 60s spent their early pioneer years in a sod house. Upon their arrival at the new homestead, the first family dwelling might have been little more than a dugout, a windowless space scooped from the side of a hill, with some boards, brush, and sod for a roof. The move to a sod house above ground was cause for celebration, despite the dirt floor and dark interior.

These marvelous geographic expedients—walls constructed from large blocks of sod and covered with rafters overlaid with more grass and sod—made for warmth in the winter and coolness in the summer. They could be as primitive or as elegant as a family had the wherewithal to construct. Some were a single room with a lean-to attached as shelter for animals. Others boasted three or four rooms. Occasionally a "soddy" even had a loft or second story and substituted real glass for the common isinglass

windows. Most were rudimentary, with little natural light, an earthy mustiness that lingered in the air, and an unpleasant tendency to leak during wet weather. At best, they meant crowded family quarters, where women tried to squeeze in treasured possessions carried from the East and to reconstruct some semblance of family life.

Women learned how to manage a family in tight spaces, when they traveled west in Conestoga wagons and other constricted conveyances. With all the family and its belongings jammed into the "prairie schooner," women quickly saw the folly of clinging to heavy dressers, chairs, and trunks. Great distances, long weeks of travel, and an uneven route wearied even the strongest draft animals. More than one family left a prized chiffonnier or wedding bed by the side of the road or traded it for supplies at some town along the route. Still, women clung to their furnishings when possible, in the hope that each would add to the home ahead.

The little sod house gave slight relief from the wagon, or, in later decades, the uncomfortable boxcars of an emigrant train. Somehow a pump organ here, a rocking chair there hardly sufficed for home. There was little space to cook, to eat, to play, to sleep. Families of six or eight, sometimes ranging in age from the newest infant to an elderly grandmother, lived together in forced intimacy. Women chafed under the close arrangements, as they watched families trying to live peaceably in one or two rooms. The added irritations of insects bursting forth from sod walls or errant cattle crashing through sod roofs did little to keep spirits high. Harmony often wilted in the face of long winter days of confinement or soggy spring days of house-drenching rain. Winter meant blinding blizzards and great drifts of snow. Spring meant hordes of insects, towering thunderstorms, and flash floods. Summer meant drought and suffocating prairie fires. Fall brought cooling winds and the knowledge that the seasons would only start over again. Most women countered the daunting environment with decorator touches, especially gardens. Patches of green vegetables, rose-colored hollyhocks, rows of potted plants, and a birdhouse or two did much to brighten the family home during the first lean years.

As farmers, men and women of the prairies labored intently to carve out a successful agrarian life. Throughout the 1860s and 1870s, windmills, hand pumps, farm equipment, and barbed wire dotted America's vast prairie space. The cycles of planting and harvesting, increasingly dependent on an expanding selection of farm inventions, shaped the lives of the family and the numerous single women who headed homesteads on their own. Whether women worked in the fields, drove the tractors, cooked in the kitchen, or (more typically) did all these things, their labor was central to the success of the family farm. In addition, it was often the wife who managed the family finances and it was she who decided when the couple might risk the expenditure of a new thresher or another eighty acres.

Small wonder that women valued the social interludes that marked a break in the farming routines. Church gatherings, whether held outdoors or in a crude building, meant more than prayer and hymns. Before and after the services, homesteaders enjoyed the chance for a visit with far-flung neighbors. Other events, such as quilting bees, church suppers, and community dances gave the families an opportunity to indulge in a welcome change from the isolation of farm living. Preparations for the Fourth of July or a local wedding also ranked as festive times, when women in an area gathered for work with a social flavor. Occasions of sickness and death also brought neighbor women together for less happy work, as families reached out to those in distress.

All these varied experiences demonstrated the vigor of isolated women in seeking each other's company. Social occasions drawn from the routines of life encouraged settlers to establish more formal organizations. Sewing groups evolved into literary and discussion clubs. Women, coming out of the Grange tradition of the 1870s, heightened their awareness of the political issues central to a farming community. By the 1890s and early 1900s, women's clubs had become fixtures in the West. Obviously, club organization proved easier for the urban women of the West than for their rural counterparts. Nonetheless, women of both the rural and urban worlds showed themselves adept at finding support and purpose in formal and informal organization. Western women transformed isolation into companionship and action.

Some people tell it like this:

The Gowan family left from St. Louis in 1846. They were going to the Willamette Valley in Oregon, where, Mr. Gowan had heard, there was rich farmland for the taking and forests thick with timber.

The Gowan's only child, Rebecca, was ten years old and curious. While her father and mother prepared the wagon for "jump off," Rebecca rushed to finish her chores, then darted along the street sticking her head in at the gunsmith and saddlery shops, and watching the men and women bustle in and out of the Radnor Hotel. Some days she sat on the docks watching steamboats struggle away from the levee, and labor up the Missouri, stuffed with emigrants, mules, horses, mule-killer carts, blacks, Indians, mountain men, gamblers, and traders.

Rebecca was too young to realize it, but the day her family boarded the boat, she was in the company of other travelers who, unlike her, would be remembered by name: Philip St. George Cooks, J. W. Abert, George Ruxton, and Francis Parkman. They were the ones who observed the West and returned to talk about what they had seen; she was, although she didn't know it on this day, one of those who was to leave not just the East, but her culture, her religion, her family.

When she was a grown woman, married to Turning Wolf, Rebecca could not remember every detail of how it had happened. Her father had bought a cow. She could not remember why. It seemed foolish to buy a cow in Ft. Laramie when you were going all the way to the ocean. But he had bought a cow and they were camped, with others, off a trail in an open ravine.

Only they weren't directly with the others. Her mother had said she wanted some privacy, so the three of them had moved further upstream, around a little bend to camp beneath a small copse of trees that whispered in the wind. She remember that sound perfectly. She remembered looking out toward the southwest over the prairie.

The cow had wandered away and her father had gone to find it. Just as he came back—or because he came back?—the Crow had swarmed up ravine and the Lakota thundered down ravine and Rebecca and her mother and father were caught in the middle. Her mother was shot through the heart, by what Rebecca later learned was a Crow arrow, and just as Turning Wolf had tossed her up over the back of his pony, she saw her father with a Crow arrow sticking from his stomach.

He was reaching toward her, as if to say, "Wait, just a minute, I had something to tell you...."

She had cried out, "Daddy!" That word she still remembered, and she knew he had wanted to save her.

*He could not have known that Turning Wolf, the Lakota, was sav-
ing her, though it must have looked as if he were stealing her away.
Turning Wolf had thrown her over the back of his horse, with her
long blond hair streaming out behind, like another tail in the wind
of escape from the Crow party.*

*As a grown woman—called Tashnatoka, and as Turning Wolf's
wife, she remembered her own fear of that day. She harbored an
intense hatred for the Crow. Enemies, and double enemies for what
they had done to her mother and father.*

*Perhaps her parents' spirits knew how happy she now was; per-
haps they recognized their grandsons walking beside Turning Wolf
along the river bank.*

*In those first days of captivity, when she refused to eat, he had
called his sisters to come sit by her; when some of the women spat at
her, he had been the one to chide them, "She is a child." He had
instructed his mother to teach her: cooking and tanning, sewing the
skins, setting up the teepee, swaddling the babies, and he had
enjoined his nieces to speak to her in the tongue, slowly, so she
could learn.*

*One day, four years later, when she still struggled between yearn-
ing for the white world and delight in her new home, she recalled a
day early in her captivity: Tashnawambli was teaching her to tan a
hide. As she worked, she noticed that Turning Wolf watched. When
she glanced up at him, she saw on his face a bewildered gaze. It was
as if he were watching an animal—in the tender, curious way she
had noticed among the Lakota. When he looked at her like this, she
felt he was aware that she was a person, a being, sacred.*

*Two years later, they married. On the first day, he began to teach
her. His words flowed out, as if they had been dammed up for many
months. He could not show her enough: this is the rain crow, this is
the deer—but she is female and pregnant, you can tell by the way
the tracks press into the earth, and we would not hunt her. This is
primrose, wild beet—the mule deer like it, and the birds eat its seed,
and when it is in the first year we boil and eat it too. He could not
seem to teach her enough. And he was proud of her courage, the
way she kept silent and absorbed what he said; she saw too that he
was enchanted by her skin, her eyes.*

She could not resist his gentle way; by the time they married, she loved and understood his people and knew that given a chance she would never return to the white world. Her eyes would always spill with grief when she thought of her parents, but Turning Wolf's people had become her own.

Her life was physically hard, especially now: they seemed always to be running from the whites who were intimidating them constantly and killing the buffalo.

Against this harrassment, Tashnatoka took delight in the peace and demand of normal chores. When she gathered firewood in the early mist and discovered a wild rose bush or when she heard the curlews call, or watched the glisten of a snake through the brush, or lay under the thick buffalo robes next to Turning Wolf, with her sons nearby, she was content. She had stepped through a veil to the other side, to the Lakota world and she wanted to stay. With the new language, in this new place, she could now recognize the track of the antelope, the scat of bear, the smell of elk, the dash of rabbit. She was at ease on the earth instead of afraid of it, as she remembered being before the Crow killed her parents. Her eyes were capable and her heart ready for peace—just when there was to be no peace. She held these moments so she could feel whole, and she tried to ignore the nagging sense that this life, these people she loved, her people, were being erased from the land.

The arrogant behavior of the whites confounded her. Had her mother and father been arrogant? She did not remember them being so; they had encouraged her curiosity, had always, as much as she could recall, treated everyone with respect.

Still, she felt responsible because of her white skin, blonde hair, stubby features—of which she could not rid herself, no matter how long she soaked in the sun or how hard she scrubbed her hair in the river.

When she walked as a Lakota, in the gatherings of the whites, she wondered at the stupidity of these white people. They lacked curiosity; they were afraid of the world; they could speak no Lakota; they treated strangers as enemies. Their barbarism toward others and toward the animals and the land flowed from the East like a flood.

Ten years after hearing that Rebecca had been taken by Turning Wolf, Reverend and Mrs. Jeremiah Stockton learned of a white woman living among the Indians. It was said she might be the Gowan girl.

"I just know it's her, John. I just know it in my heart." Mrs. Stockton's missionary zeal glowed from her face. With the determination of a self-righteous heart, she convinced her husband to rescue Goldilocks from the bears.

It seemed too easy when they simply ran across her near the fort where she was walking with a group of Indians. They had envisioned themselves searching from village to village, braving the savages, to find the girl—who would run to their arms, tears of gratitude and relief streaming down her face.

This woman didn't even look at them. She walked by, talking and laughing with her friends. She seemed...well...content, happy even. The Stocktons turned and followed them, and when they drew even with them, Mrs. Stockton caught the white one by the arm.

At the touch, Tashnatoka wheeled around, prepared to defend herself. Mrs. Stockton jumped back. Tashnatoka glared at her.

"Why have you touched me?" She demanded in Lakota.

Mrs. Stockton did not understand.

"Ah...I am Mrs. Stockton, the reverend's wife." She indicated her husband. "We have come to rescue you. To bring you back to your people."

The woman's words sounded familiar, but jumbled. Tashnatoka stared at her silly dress with its wide skirt, tight and restrictive about the waist and bodice. Her hair was unnatural in arrangement and her forward behavior embarrassing.

She looked directly into the white woman's eyes, hoping she would go away.

"Rebecca?" Mrs. Stockton spoke in a whisper, but Tashnatoka heard the name her parents had called her.

Why did this woman know her white name? And why would she feel free to use it? Tashnatoka felt ashamed, and angered.

"Rebecca, dear." Mrs. Stockton reached out again.

They said later that Tashnatoka stabbed Mrs. Stockton in the arm. They said the Gowan girl had gone savage. In truth, Tashnatoka only slapped her with the flat of her palm. She slapped her because this missionary in her blind zeal wanted to touch and rearrange and intrude. Slapped her because the woman was an affront to Tashnatoka's life and her people, her children and her husband, to her land. Slapped her out of shame that this rude woman who did not know where in the world she was, had skin the color of Tashnatoka's own.

WHITE PIONEERS

*H*ow could twenty-two-year-old Charlotte Townsend of Newton, Massachusetts, possibly have known about the life of a pioneer woman, even as late as 1910? She married a homesteader, Delbert Theall, who had left his acres in the far West and journeyed back to Massachusetts to ask the woman he had met once to become his bride. Years later, she still wondered why she had done it. They left from her mother's home on the day of the wedding, caught the afternoon train, and headed for the West. Delbert, a native of St. John, New Brunswick, insisted they push on past the American plains to Alberta. Charlotte willingly moved on with her new husband, completely unaware of what lay in store.

The city of Calgary seemed interesting and not so different from home. But when they moved beyond the city and arrived at the tar paper shack somewhat vaguely near the hamlet of Keoma, Charlotte could not believe her eyes. No amenities graced this first home. There was no running water, only a creek far behind the shack and down an incline. No neighbors came to greet her. As far as her eye could travel, she saw nothing but the flat open spaces.

When her first child was born, Charlotte happily went into the hospital at Calgary, where she got some respite from the isolation at the little house. Its remoteness seemed to grow when she returned with her baby daughter. Each morning Delbert left for the fields, bringing in two small pails of water from the creek before he left. Charlotte used the little water supply within the first hour each morning and spent the rest of the day hauling more and more pails for the baby, for the cooking, for the washing.

When she could stand the loneliness no longer, she packed a

noon day meal and dressed herself in Delbert's trousers so as not to have a flapping skirt that would scare the horses, near wild and only recently captured off the prairie. Properly attired, she set forth and carried her infant daughter a mile across the open land to spend some time with Delbert. He worked alongside a Norwegian farmer, whose non-English speaking wife brought her youngsters to the same lunch spot. There the two women sat locked in a silent companionship, watching their children at play and their husbands at work, raising rye to be made into whiskey. This mute communication became Charlotte's only social connection to another woman the entire time she lived on the prairie.

Perhaps for sociability the Thealls could count the threshing gangs that crisscrossed the area at harvest time. These men moved from one homestead to another, hiring out their labor to the strapped farmers. But Charlotte did not view the arrival of these visitors as pleasurable, for if a gang arrived on Saturday for a Monday harvest, she did a full day of extra cooking to feed the crew three meals on Sunday.

Of course, the inevitable events of prairie living took over this tiny group. The Norwegian farmer died in a frightful tractor accident. His family packed their belongings and disappeared—the Thealls never knew anything of the fate of the young widow and her children.

As for Charlotte—finally, the task of dragging the buckets of water took its toll. She wrenched her back so badly, she lay in agonizing pain for days. It proved an injury from which she never fully recovered, but it sparked her determination that the Thealls should leave the sweeping prairie homesteading life. Delbert, weary from the constant battle against prairie fires and the repeated destruction of the crop from hailstorms, agreed. First, they retreated to the city of Calgary, but finally a desire to be again amidst their own led them back to rural Massachusetts, where they lived out their years on a small farm.

She called him "Papa," he called her "Mama." They raised two children and lost a third to the diphtheria epidemic of 1919. With their son and daughter grown, they opened their home to foster children and cared for nearly two dozen over a span of fifteen years. When he died suddenly in 1951, Charlotte seemed most of all surprised; clearly, she had never imagined life without Papa.

Over the years in Massachusetts, Charlotte's "frontier life" ebbed away to memory, renewed when her foster children and grandchildren would demand to see her old Alberta photo album. There was the tar paper shack, the prairie, the Norwegian husband atop his tractor, the Indians on the streets of Calgary. Among the characters stood the youthful Mama and Papa, smiling and bold, undaunted by the incredible stark scenes around them. Charlotte would look at the fading photographs and tell the stories of each again and again.

Just the mention of Calgary started her off on how much it meant to get away from Keoma and take a trip into town. Perhaps her favorite tale was about the day she had a lunch of shrimp and cabbage salad at the home of a Calgary woman she barely knew. Charlotte, accustomed to the dreary fare out on the prairie, was so famished for the taste of a fresh vegetable that she fell on her food and wolfed it down without a word of conversation. How she laughed at herself later, laughed about her hunger, her lack of social grace.

Underneath ran a small current of pain and some annoyance at a husband who seemed oblivious to the deprivations of their existence. She shared little in their decision making, even accepting his startling announcement that they would follow the Christian Science religion. Delbert had seen Mary Baker Eddy's *Science and Health With Key to the Scriptures* in the window of a Calgary reading room and brought it home, declaring that from that time forward the Thealls would be members of the Scientist church, and so they were for the remainder of their long lives.

The saga of Charlotte Townsend Theall captured in life what W. H. D. Koerner hoped to convey on canvas. However, Charlotte Theall lived that pioneer existence with an essence and a grittiness that Koerner missed in his saccharine portrait. She showed plenty of Koerner courage and fortitude. Beyond that, no passive, docile wife, she knew how to express her resistance to and rejection of a life that wore at her husband's enormous strength, limited her children's social options, and nearly broke her own health.

In the prairie tradition, Charlotte was an American pioneer woman, but she refused to remain one. Part of her courage took shape in the way she managed the extremes of homesteading life. Part of her courage showed itself in her ability to turn away from that life when it proved too brutal, too lonely, and too far from kith and kin. Charlotte Townsend Theall found her personal courage, because, for good and for ill, pioneer life marked her being. The prairie years gave her voice and shaped her womanhood.

She closed her eyes, and then opened them again. It was still there at the top of the falls. Through her husband's shirt, the pebbles along the creek bank poked into the tender skin of her back. She rubbed back and forth against the ground, liking the feel of it. She looked up at this being. It had a head—that was all it had—a good twenty feet high, with enormous eyes. Its angular nose jutted out over the falls, except when it turned to face her, as it did now. From the front, its nose created a line down the center of its face. She had once seen a face like it in a picture of a place called Easter Island.

She crossed one ankle over her knee, her arms behind her head. It stared at her and frowned.

"What's wrong?" she asked. "Do you wish I wouldn't wear men's clothes."

"I don't care about men's clothes." It scowled, but its voice was gentle.

"What do you care about?"

"I care about you."

"I don't understand."

"You've got to listen. You're not listening."

"To what?"

"To yourself. You're thinking about clothes and about dinner and about what they think. They will suck you dry. They will slurp you up like a raw egg. Climb up here. Come up here to me. Come...or run back to your husband."

Its voice echoed inside and outside her head. She had heard it for months, but this was the first time she had seen its source.

It turned away, its nose protruding over the falls. She laughed, its nose looked funny, but it turned back so angrily that she stopped abruptly. A mist from the water drifted over her face, leaving a sparkling dew across her chest and thighs. She closed her eyes again, wishing she could lay there forever.

"Decide," it said.

Her body carried her effortlessly over the rocks and through the arches of thick willow and aspen. She had been up since midnight. Now it was dawn, and they would wonder where she was. They still weren't used to her going like this, and they never liked it.

Her husband watched her approach. In men's clothes again, she was bright-eyed, exuberant in the joy of her lunancy. He saw that they were watching her from the other wagons; she was oblivious.

"John! John!" she called to him, waving her arms. "I've been to the falls. Such a beautiful morning!"

The journey had been her idea from the beginning. In fact, all of it had been her idea: to marry, to use the money from their parents to come West. Now here they were, camped along the Snake River, headed for Oregon. He felt pulled into a spate. He would not have chosen to come West, but she was irresistible to him; he couldn't say no.

In her spells, like today, she talked incessantly about their new home. They would farm in the Willamette Valley; they would have scads of children, they would live in a white clapboard house with a porch—but he saw, the longer he lived with her, that she would lean heavily on him, that her ideas flowed faster than her hands. Even her letters home, dozens of them from this trip alone, lay half-finished in the chest in the wagon.

"Byron." She announced.

"Please, Cilla, not poetry again. Not before breakfast. The others don't like it."

"But it's perfect. Perfect. Oh, I wish you could have seen the falls. I wish you could have seen what was up there." Her eyes glinted.

"What was it..?"

"And you know, they say he kept a bear for a pet at Cambridge— and we are going to see bears when we get to Oregon."

"Who...?"

She started in before he could finish.

"'In my youth's summer . . .' I am in my youth's summer!" She hugged him.

"Please, Cilla, not here, not in front of everyone."

"Oh, they don't give a fig. They like to see us loving each other." She grabbed him and hugged him, then turned to the women at the fire who were staring.

> *"'In my youth's summer I did sing of One*
> *The wandering outlaw of his own dark mind;*
> *Again I seize the theme then but begun*
> *And bear it...'*

"See!" she laughed at her husband. "See, B E A R.

"'And bear it with me, as the rushing wind
Bears the clouds onward: In that tale I find
The furrows of long thought . . .'

"Bears and furrows. It's a sign. Oregon and farming." Her voice was beginning to break. She had tears in her eyes.

"'Perchance my heart and harp have lost a string
And both may jar: It may be, that in vain
I would essay as I have sung to sing;
Yet, though a dreary strain, to this I cling;
So that it wean me from the weary dream
Of selfish grief or gladness—so it fling
Forgetfulness around me . . .'"

Her voice trailed off. The others turned away in embarrassment. John watched the tears stream down her cheeks and drop onto his shirt that she had taken off the hook in the dark night to go running up the narrow canyon to the falls. He regarded her with love, but she was not well, and when he found her late next afternoon at the bottom of the falls, below the giant boulder that jutted partway over the high pool, he thought, even in his grief, that maybe it was better this way.

BLACK PIONEERS

After 1870, those sweeping Great Plains, where life came with hard edges, became the domain of the American farmer. In less than twenty years, an agrarian explosion soaked up more than one billion acres of land west of the Mississippi River. Americans and immigrants alike defined "opportunity" as the chance to claim and work a western homestead.

Following the Civil War, more and more black Americans turned their faces toward the new life they perceived to be in the West. Perhaps close to 40,000 African Americans joined the westward migrations; at least 15,000 moved into Kansas. Somehow this great collection of American farm families seems to be missing in the large picture of the western experience.

Anxious to remove themselves from the unpleasant reminders of their slavery and secure in their agricultural knowledge, former slaves looked to the American West as the place they might capture that justice and freedom always denied them. After 1877, for black families, the realities of life in the South included the growing indifference of national leaders and the increasing dangers of local "home rule."

As blacks pulled up stakes and headed out of the deep South, white Southerners used various strategies to thwart the migrations. These ranged from arrest to intimidation to murder. The lure of land ownership, a promise that had died in the postwar South, and the chance for a somewhat better life maintained the determination of black families in the face of terrifying southern pressures.

The latter part of the 1870s saw the pace of the exodus pick up, fueled by a general poor economy in the South and the sad realization that black freedoms had no southern prospects. Although all settlers faced physical hardship in relocating to the West, black Americans endured a larger dose than others. Strapped by limited means, exposed to the elements, faced with hunger, harassed at every turn, the migrants pressed on.

African Americans, who came to be known as the "Exodusters," found enough of a new life to organize and manage their own communities, five in Kansas alone. Of these, Nicodemus, Kansas, founded in 1877, was best known, especially to African Americans who used it as their beacon to freedom.

African American homesteaders also relied on the sod house for a home. Like their white neighbors, often several generations lived together in one small space. Their hope for social, economic, and political equality did not materialize as fully as they dreamed, but for many life as a homesteader ranked above the grinding poverty of those who stayed behind in the plantation South. Black families took on not only the burdens of homesteading, but individuals often held other jobs to supplement slim family profits. Husbands went to nearby towns to work at urban jobs,

while black women added domestic service to white families and washing and ironing to their labor.

In the Exoduster migrations, blacks demonstrated one way in which African Americans of the post-Civil War years responded to untenable living conditions and exercised control over their lives. So often written out of the western historical record, black families sought improvement and prosperity for their children, as did other pioneers. They placed their emphasis, whether in urban or rural settings, on striving for a middle-class American life, always hoping that equality and justice would be available to their children through their own hard work. To that end, they worked, dressed, and lived to accommodate the standards of a dominant white society.

That their endeavors met with such a cold reception in the nineteenth century foretold of events of the twentieth century. For example, in this story of the West, many Americans have forgotten the strong family emphasis African Americans brought to the experience. Especially neglected have been accounts of individual black women and the heroic dimensions of their lives. Aunt Clara Brown, who used the gold rush in Colorado as her ticket to the West, became a noted entrepreneur, and financed the passage of more than two dozen relatives to the West; hers is only one story of courage. Era Bell Thompson, a small child amidst a sea of white playmates in North Dakota, is only one example of fortitude. Chloe Flipper, wife of West Point's first black graduate whom the military cashiered under questionable charges, is only one wife among thousands who witnessed the way that injustice seared her family.

Throughout the late nineteenth and early twentieth centuries, African Americans found various ways to use the opportunity of the West for the betterment of black citizens in many regions of the United States. Black Americans in the West often reached out beyond their own families to extend the hand of fellowship and help to others in their communities. The Jubilee Singers of Tennessee traveled the West, giving vocal performances to raise money for black education. Black women launched benevolent groups, especially within their churches, in all western locations and pursued the issues of social reform through womanhood with a vigor that paralleled and sometimes exceeded other western females. Beginning in 1896, the National Association of Colored Women affiliated with aid societies and clubs across the West and always supported the advancement of black Americans. The existence of black neighborhoods in a number of towns—Leavenworth, Denver, Cheyenne, Austin, Helena—suggests that the western experience did not belong exclusively to any one cultural group. The life stories of black women reflect the hope and expectations they held for themselves, their families, and all African Americans.

They captured Susanna Reece and her two children at the Alabama line. "Nigger bastards," they shouted, forcing them into a huddle in the grove of trees. The bigger one, Lander, had a whip; he

cracked it from where he sat on his saddle. "What do you think yer doing, Susanna? Trying to run." His horse skittered each time he snapped the whip, but he paid no attention.

"Nig-ger bastards! Susanna and her two bas-tards." He drew the words out, and laughed. "Where ya gonna run to, huh?" The sound of the whip exploded in the air. "Off to Kan-sas? Off to free-dom?" He laughed again and nodded at his companion, Johnathan, who was grunting and calling out after his friend, like an echo: "Yah! Niggers! Yah! We'll show you some re-construction!"

Susanna watched them carefully. She had raised Lander herself, in his folks' big white house near Crooked Oak. The mix of excitement and fear in his eyes was familiar to her. It was a bad combination.

Susanna stared straight at Lander. Willing him to look at her, she began to hum softly, barely audible, as she put an arm around each of her children, Mary, thirteen and Joshua, fifteen. She drew them close against her, all the time watching the two on the horses.

Mmm Hmm, O what preachin! O what preachin!
O what preachin over me, over me!

"Hey Johnathan!" Lander was shouting even though he was mounted next to his friend. "Let's have some fun with Mary before we take 'em back." He turned to face Susanna squarely, "Back to work, like they's supposed to be." He grinned at the other boy.

"Yeah Lander, let's give her a poke she'll never forget."

Before Susanna could stop him, Joshua had broken from her grasp and leaped forward toward Lander. He reached up, grabbing at the whip, but missed. Almost in the same instant, Johnathan struck him across the back of the head with his rifle, and Joshua fell to the ground.

"Oh, Joshua's brave. Ohhhh." Lander slid off his horse. "Johnathan, this boy done attacked me. This brave nigger boy come right at me!" He pulled his own rifle from its scabbard and, shouting "Ohhhh Joshua's brave, Joshua's brave," struck with two swift movements, smashing both of Joshua's legs below the knees. Johnathan laughed wildly, intoxicated by the power of his friend.

Just as Lander raised his rifle to strike again, Susanna stepped in front of him and grasped the weapon. She looked him in the eyes. She had raised so many spoiled white children, but this was a bad son of good parents, a coward who committed his mean acts in the secrecy of a shed, or the isolation of a far field. A bead of sweat trickled down his forehead; he was perspiring from the exciting exertion of his own violence.

Susanna held his gaze, compelling him by her presence, by her calm, to look at her.

"What'd YOU want, Susanna, you black bitch! Some of the same?" He spit in her face, but she held her ground and did not flinch. "I could give you what I gave him! Yer supposed to be working! Working my land!" He was screaming now, a high pitched, nasal screech.

Susanna studied every detail of his face: the thin brows, the narrow ridge of nose, the lanky blond hair, the pimpled white skin. He had been a sweet baby. His parents, for their kind, were gentle people, though they had sold her other daughters and her husband away without a second thought. She looked at this boy, wondering what

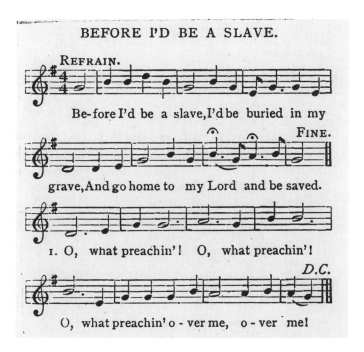

BEFORE I'D BE A SLAVE.

Be-fore I'd be a slave, I'd be buried in my

grave, And go home to my Lord and be saved.

1. O, what preachin'! O, what preachin'!

O, what preachin' o - ver me, o - ver me!

had happened to the spirit of the child in him. Where had it gone? Did the hate and the cruelty run in the sap of the trees of this land? Did it rise up from the sources of the rivers? Run in the juices of the fruit and the meat they ate? Was it some illness, like a plague, among them?

The spit ran down over her eyes and dropped onto her cheeks, but she stood, unflinching, staring straight at his ugly face and she saw that, slowly, fear was filling his eyes like steam rises up in the cold air. The scared little boy was surfacing in the face of the full-grown, impudent body. Susanna felt her stomach turn; she was sickened by this contortion in front of her. He wanted to look away, but she held him, staring deep into his faded blue eyes, slowly twisting the gun out of his hand.

"Mister Johnathan, You done had yer fun; now it's enough. You go on back home now. I bet your Daddy don't even know what yer doing."

Lander blushed, his pasty skin turning a mottled pink. His head dropped. Susanna tossed the rifle into the bushes.

"What'dya...," Johnathan started to shout—then, seeing his friend was cowed before the black woman, and having no courage of his own, spurred his horse round and rode off.

Susanna turned and kneeled beside her son. She slid her arms slowly under his neck and thighs and pulled him gently up to her. He winced with the pain. Holding her boy, she turned back to Lander.

"You better git on after your friend." Then she turned her back to him, her courage evident in every line of her shoulders, in the tendons of her neck, in the strain of her muscles. Carrying her son, she

walked off toward the brush where her daughter was watching. As she moved, she sang.

O, what mourning! O, what mourning!
O, what mourning over me, over me!

Susanna and her daughter made a litter of shirts and pants and carried Joshua all the way to Nebraska.

Years later, at home on the Nebraska plains, Susanna would sometimes blurt out to no one in particular, "A soddy! Nebraska! I never even heard of this place before. Ain't no more trees 'n you can count on yer hand."

She took in laundry, her son farmed, and for cash they sang. They sang at the funerals and the weddings of the white citizens in the nearby town. But at home, they sang for themselves. Susanna's strong mellow voice rose out over the land, night or day, like the gold slant of light on an early fall afternoon.

O, what singing! O, what singing!
O, what singing over me, over me.
Before I'd be a slave, I'd be buried in my grave.
And go home to my Lord and be saved.

2

Immigrant Women

*T*he year is 1870. Three people: an English woman about thirty years old, her daughter, ten, and her son, a boy of twelve. They are standing on the quay in Liverpool. The quay is packed with people surrounded by bundles and boxes. Children are crying, and shouting in a dozen or more languages. This is the exit port for America.

The woman is nervous. She is pacing back and forth near their luggage. Her husband, a shoemaker, had left her five years earlier; it was then she determined that she would go to America. After her husband left, she convinced the Boss that she could do the work herself.

"How're ya gonna work with the waxed thread, Lizbeth?" he'd asked.

"I can do it. I'm strong enough." She stared him in the eye and he saw her determination. He laughed.

"Ok. We'll give it a try."

She had taken the position her husband had held, cutting and finishing the heavy sewing at the factory, then bringing home the lighter binding and sewing to do at home. She became like two people. The boy watched his sister while his mother was in the factory, and they all worked at light sewing when she was home. In five years, she had saved enough for passage for two of them. She was strong from working the machines, but the work had made her bitter.

"The boat won't leave for another two hours yet."

"Are you sure, Mama?" the boy asks. He is both frightened and excited by the confusion and by the idea of going to America.

"Yes. Now run back home and bring the envelope from the little drawer near the bed. It's got Mrs. Carston's cousin's address on it. Mrs. Blackwell will let you in and your sister and I will wait here."

"Are you sure, Mama?"

She kisses him on the cheek; the show of affection makes him buoyant and he runs off on the errand.

He finds her in Salt Lake City twelve years later, when he is twenty-four. He never mentions how she abandoned him that day. Somehow he had followed her reasoning, had understood her greed to get away, even though many tearful times he had envisioned how, as soon as he left to bring the envelope, she and his sister had boarded the boat and sailed out of harbor.

For her part, when the mother looks at the son, her heart twists in her chest. She had converted, had found a people to live amongst; her daughter had married. She has a comfortable life, but she suffers from chronic insomnia—and when her death comes, she welcomes it. The New World never fulfilled what her dream had promised.

The European immigrant woman endured more than an uncertain trek from east to west. Double jeopardy marked her pioneer life. She often left a hostile home world to enter an equally uninviting new community. Her dress, her language, her religion—all these placed the foreign-born woman immigrant at a disadvantage. The story of her survival and success in the American West undoubtedly can be attributed to her ability to mix her old heritage with her new.

Powerful social forces fueled the movement of Europeans to America's shores and impelled thousands to continue inland to take up the life of the American homesteader. After the Civil War, deteriorating economic conditions in a number of European countries and the promise of prosperity in a new land sparked the migrations of Irish, German, Russian, Swedish, Norwegian, Danish, and Jewish peoples to the United States. If the sorry economic condition at home did not inspire Europeans to leave, the regular political upheavals, religious persecutions, and military skirmishes convinced the reluctant migrant. Some wanted to escape the czar, some the king, some the queen.

The women came for every possible reason. They followed husbands, they supported families, they sought husbands, they longed for adventure, they yielded to colonization efforts of the western states, the railroads, and the U.S. government. All wanted the chance to own land, a dazzling 160 acres under the Homestead Act of 1862.

Some moved in groups and formed national enclaves in western states. Minnesota and the Dakotas, as well as Utah, welcomed groups of Scandinavian farmers. These newcomers, especially the women, relied on the support of common church groups and women's social organizations. In Utah, immigrants, particularly Scandinavians, who migrated to join the Church of Jesus Christ of Latter-day Saints, melded into a carefully organized structure that expected and responded to national differences among new residents. The story of these immigrant Mormons was not without its conflict and controversy, but it was always framed by a strong sense of family and community.

Less easy a transition awaited the thousands of immigrant families who went to a rural homestead and set up their new farms. Women living in these conditions felt the personal isolation. Cut off from their own cultural group, alone for days on end, they had

few chances to mix with neighbors, and typically their English language skills lagged behind those of husbands and children who moved more freely in the new community.

For many families the sudden assault of a new environment was nothing compared to the shock created by the clash between a European way of life and American middle-class values. Native-born white Americans had expressed an intense concern about the acculturation of immigrant groups since the 1840s and sought ways through education, religion, and popular culture to "Americanize" recent arrivals. White women expected foreign-born women to join in the cause of "civilizers" and protectors of the home. This expectation intensified for women in the West, a region that eastern society had long looked on with suspicion for its "free and unfettered" conduct. For the foreign-born woman, already overwhelmed by change and travel, confusion and displacement, the demand to absorb some vague, uncomfortable standards that did not apply to her must have been one more painful element in the immigration process.

Even if a woman could ignore the language differences, the religious hostility, and the class differentials, there was always the merciless weather of the Great Plains to torment her. Though she might ignore or dismiss the human made aggravations, no one could overlook the persistence of the harsh climate. Summer and winter, it surrounded the immigrant with its punishing heat, brutal storms, and stereophonic winds.

Beyond these hardships, immigrants—like native-born American migrants—persevered. They did so, in part, because all these groups believed in the potential of farming. They understood the mounting human crisis created by a mushrooming industrial world that stretched from the East Coast to the West Coast, from the Canadian border to the Mexican. All people needed to eat, and these pioneers—African American, white American, recent immigrant—became part of the national undertaking to feed the multitudes. With the traditionally optimistic spirit of the agrarian, these families expected an agricultural bonanza to carry them well into the twentieth century.

Unhappily, the fickle nature of farming plagued most. Drought and poor markets, plus control by America's railroad corporations weakened the original pioneer zest that brought settlers to the prairies. Some faltered and withdrew into the cities. Other families clung to the land, despite the roller-coaster

economy. The social and economic pressures of farming led in 1869 to the organization of the Grange, which focused exclusively on the needs of the farmer. Its social and political strategies aided the farm communities, but left the fundamental problems uncorrected. By the 1880s, farm men and women again felt the need for redress of their economic difficulties and flocked into the newly formed Farmers' Alliances. These gained strength from the Dakotas to Texas, enrolling more than five million members, one fifth of whom joined the black association. In the 1890s, agrarian reform burst forth among the leaders of the Populist Party. American farm families had evolved from single pioneer units to an organized political voice.

* behind every history there is another history, and another. . . . Imagine a two-story wooden frame house on Grant Street in North Omaha, Nebraska, in the year 1917. In that year, Omaha is full of horses and wagons; in front of this particular house on Grant is the wagon of a junk dealer. The streets are narrow. This is the*

lower-class, Jewish part of town. The air smells of cabbage, fresh bread, and sweat. There are children crying and shouting. There are children coming home from unloading crates at the outdoor markets, or from selling newspapers on the street corners downtown. A trolley clangs past.

On its eastern side, Omaha is bounded by the Missouri River and the bluffs along the Iowa border above the river. To the west, the land rolls away toward Lincoln. It is hot; the air is heavy.

On Saturday afternoons a Russian Jew named Fruma sits in the white house on Grant Street and watches her son, Lazar, playing pinochle with his friends. When her friend, Shoshana, berates her for allowing him to play cards on the Sabbath, Fruma laughs good-naturedly and says, "Would you rather have them go to a bar to play?"

Fruma is a big woman, broad shouldered and full-hipped, and she is happy; she is the sort of happy that people experience when they have suffered much and have learned exactly how much each minute is worth. "Let them play," she says.

Imagine the Nebraska landscape. The earth around Omaha is dry and brown in the summer heat; the air sits on the skin. The hills roll west toward the Great American Desert. Out there are rattlesnakes, the echo of buffalo and Pawnee, the Platte River—a mile wide and an inch deep, dividing and redividing into a thousand threads. Quicksand, clumps of cottonwood, prickly pears.

Counting back from the day Fruma stands in the front room, watching her son play cards with his friends, it is only seventy-one years since Francis Parkman made his historic trip along the Oregon Trail in 1846; it is only forty-one years since the Battle of the Little Big Horn. Fruma does not know about Parkman, and would not be able to distinguish a Pawnee from a Kiowa, or Custer's face from that of any other white American male. To enthusiasts, the year 1876 commemorates the battle of the Little Big Horn. To her, 1876 is not 1876, but 5645, the year of her birth on the Horin River in Byelorussia.

Fruma is unaware of much of American history. This is not because she is uneducated. She speaks and reads Yiddish and Russian. She reads Hebrew and knows some Polish. Through night courses, she is rapidly closing in on English as her fourth language.

No, if Fruma goes for a picnic west of Omaha, to the rolling hills between her home and Lincoln, she does not think of the days when Omaha was the West, or of the jump-off sites of Independence and Westport, of riverboats on the Missouri, of covered wagons and the Oregon Trail, of handcarts, of the monotony of the plain, of the vast expanse of sands, or the turbid waters of the Platte, or the thick mud in the wet seasons in the Great American Desert. She has no visceral sense of the American West. She has not read Blue Hotel, and she has not traveled far out of Omaha.

She reminisces instead about her mother and father and about her own childhood, about David-Horodok, a small town in the heart of Polesye on the Horin River that flowed through the middle of town. She thinks of thick forests and broad swamplands, and of Mordechai Selig's orchard in Tchipovski Street and the dirt path to the Kvuarsker windmill and onto the marshes. She thinks of the open markets, of the meat hanging on hooks, the butchers with their giant cleavers, of the transport belinas on which her husband worked, and of the other ships and barges plying back and forth to the Pripyet and from there to the Dneiper. She thinks of the Amalia Hotel and the Great Synagogue.

And she thinks of the 1905 revolution and the pogrom when a man named Zuchter axed to death all but one of the Horenstein family.

She thinks of the cobblers and the tailors and the hatmakers and the watchmakers, the smiths, the teamsters, and the hasids; and now, in 1917, she listens intently to the talk of yet another revolution, because she knows David-Horodok will not escape the conflagration, and she knows, with a particular knowledge, that the Jews of David-Horodok will not escape unharmed.

She worries. But she hopes and somehow believes, that the ones she knew there in David Horodok will perservere and survive. This belief is to her credit. She cannot, thank G-d, imagine thirty-nine years into the future; she cannot conceive of what is beyond imagining.

So, she sits with her friend Shoshana, and remembers; and sometimes in the silence of an October afternoon, she remembers her betrothal.

One October day in 1894, Shleme went to the Slitsky's house to propose to the eldest sister. But it was Fruma who opened the door—and Shleme was smitten.

He told the girls' father: "I want Fruma instead."

"But I don't want to marry him!" she cried out.

Her father turned and slapped her so hard across the face that she staggered back, against the wall.

Seventeen years later, Shleme and Fruma lived in a fine house on the Horin River, with a Russian maid named Baboyeho, a Jewish maid, whose name is forgotten, and seven children. Beryl, who was never mentioned for the grief that even the sound of his name elicited, died when he was two, and another baby had died before he could be named.

Shleme was a shipbuilder. He and his men constructed the high-bellied belinas, *twenty* sajen *long, three* sajen *wide, and two* arshin *high; they also built the barges that carried firewood to the towns along the rivers as far as Kiev. In the summer, Shleme watched the ships he had built labor up the Dneiper hauling grains, and in the fall he saw them burdened with salt from the Ukraine, inching upstream to David-Horodok.*

At home, the children chattered and studied, and Shmuel, just sixteen, remembered his father's oath that none of his sons would serve the czar. Every Jew in Russia knew the czar's unwritten policy on Jews: to assimilate one third, to starve to death one third, and to allow one third to emigrate. The czar's special military tactic was part of the policy of assimilation: young Jewish men were forced to eat unclean foods, to abandon the Sabbath, to desecrate the holy days.

In 1912 the family made a decision. Shleme and Shmuel left in the night, made their way across the border, into Austria, then Germany, and from there to England, where they took passage on a boat to Canada.

After a time in Canada, they received a letter from Fruma's brother, Louie Slitsky, a butcher. He wrote, "Come to me. There is work in the big meat packing plants."

Two years later, with no news of her husband except an address in a place called Omaha, Nebraska, Fruma sold everything except the family candlesticks and a few books. She boarded a train with her remaining children. At Odessa, they took passage on a ship sailing through the Black Sea, the Mediterranean, and up to Liverpool, departure point for to America.

In Liverpool, the health inspector checked them all. Last was Nachman.

"He'll never get in." The inspector turned and spoke to Fruma. "He's got trachoma. They'll let you and the others in, but not him."

Fruma thanked him and herded her children ahead of her toward the boat to America.

They landed in Philadelphia.

I try to imagine Fruma looking around her as they debarked, hearing the sounds of English for only the second time. The first American she would have seen clearly would have been the health inspector, checking the ears and eyes of the immigrants.

"I need to sit down," she told the children.

They watched her shuffle to a bench, sit down, and close her eyes. When she opened them, she took one deep breath, looked each of her children in the face, her gaze hesitating a moment on each, and then held out her arms.

They gathered around her, and she whispered to them in Yiddish, "Here is what we're going to do...."

I think this was Fruma's greatest moment of courage and wit. All the power she had as a protector was concentrated in this moment. This was staying or going back. This meant being a wife or a grass widow. This meant poverty or security, and though she didn't yet know it—and wouldn't know it until the 17th of the Jewish month of Av, 5710, when the good people of David-Horodok, with the black blessings of the Nazis, massacred three thousand Jews in one day— this meant life or death.

Fruma was a stranger in a strange world.

First through the gate was Lazer Mihel, holding Fagela and Basela by the hand. Then came Fruma with Buskha, last was Nachman with Hannehla. The inspector passed Lazer Mihel, Fagela, Basela, Fruma and Buskha, and then turned to Nachman and the two and one-half year-old toddler.

As the inspector raised his instrument to look, Nachman, under the baby's wrappings, jabbed her with a hat pin that he had concealed in his sleeve. The baby screamed.

The inspector jumped back. Fruma began to wave and call out. The inspector looked at the mother, waving her arms in desperation, then he looked down at the baby and Nachman. He had been dealing with immigrants all day and he was tired. Shaking his head, he waved them through—to freedom, where those children became the aunts and uncles of my husband, and where Fruma became the great-grandmother of my children.

Some women immigrated by a west to east route. More than a travel path separated their experiences from that of the east to west migrant. The slight attention Americans give to the Asian experience in the West has centered on some vague ideas about Chinese men and the building of the transcontinental railroad in the 1860s. Although treated with indifference and historical neglect, Asian women also played a role in the emergence of the West, as it is now known.

Asian women left their homelands, often without choice. Powerful economic and political forces catapulted some, without their assent, onto ships bound for the California coast. Many women had no idea where they were headed or what awaited them at the end of the tumultuous crossing. Others knew or suspected that they as single women, without the protection of families, were destined for the brothels of San Francisco. In these bordellos, Chinese women lived and worked under harsh conditions that often led to early death. After the 1880s, anti-Chinese legislation reduced the number of women arriving for prostitution. In fact,

the demographics of Chinese immigration shifted somewhat and more
women, domestic servants, or wives
of entrepreneurs arrived in the
United States. Such women slowly
moved into the Rocky Mountain
West, as overseers and business
owners extended the work region of
the Chinese.

Certainly, the migration experiences of Asian women formed few
parallels with the European. The
patterns of movement, the cultural
environment, and the women's
expectations all differed greatly
from the Caucasian women of the
West. The most singular aspect of
the arrival of the Asian immigrant
woman emerged in the contempt
and disregard with which the communities of the American West
greeted her. Perhaps no group of
women faced as much ostracization
and lack of sensitivity as did women from the Asian cultures.

The intensity of anti-Chinese sentiment, for example, made
men hesitate to bring wives and children to the United States. In
addition, anti-Chinese immigration legislation and the scant
resources of the first male Chinese immigrants made it difficult
for great numbers of women to come to the United States. When
they did, after 1880, the barriers of discrimination prompted the
Chinese to seek the security of their own neighborhoods. Anglos
regarded these sectors to be mysterious and vice-ridden. They
placed Chinese women at the center of that scenario as either
licentious, immoral prostitutes or enslaved chattel.

Although Chinese women faced many constraints and were
subjected to enforced prostitution, neither image correctly captured the development of gender within the Asian community. In

their early years in this country, Chinese women remained home-
bound, but like many other immigrant women performed low
wage jobs, while carrying out their family and domestic duties.
Chinese women, albeit behind the scenes, joined with their
fathers, husbands, and brothers to build a family economy in the
United States. They engaged in every kind of enterprise and, in
some cases, built vast family fortunes.

The Chinatown Telephone Exchange, the brainstorm of businessman Loo Kim Shu, was an example of a Chinese enterprise
that depended almost exclusively on the labor of women.
Designed in 1894 to serve as a jobber's link to the labor supply in
Chinatown, the service grew into the communications center of
the San Francisco Chinese world. As it expanded, Loo Kim Shu
shifted to all women operators, who in turn created a work
dynasty, at retirement passing their jobs to their daughters. At its
peak, the exchange handled more than 13,000 calls a day and represented an important bridge between the Chinese and Caucasian
communities. Perhaps even more important, it emerged as a hub
of Chinese culture, a means of employment for women, and a
way in which those women, living by strict gender constraints,
within an even more constraining dominant society, guaranteed a
work future for their own daughters.

Other Asian nationals also migrated to the West Coast, most
especially the Japanese. Japanese women did not arrive in signif-
icant numbers until after 1909, when an immigration arrangement between the United States and Japan allowed for female
entry. Japanese men already living in the U. S. quickly
responded to the opportunity to secure wives from the mother
country. Young Japanese women, called picture-brides from the
practice of exchanging photographs with possible suitors, left
the comfort of their own homes for the alien shores of California.
Family arrangements, economic necessity, or a sense of personal
adventure explained their willingness to make the long journey
toward matrimony with an unknown male. For some, the venture led to successful marriages, while others felt keen disap-
pointment when, face-to-face, they discovered the photograph of
the intended had been taken fifteen or twenty years previous.

With U. S. anti-Asian sentiment on the rise, these women benefitted from the close associations they had within their own ethnic community. As a group, they stayed within the confines of their own families, and when they did undertake employment outside the Japanese neighborhood, they usually worked at some form of domestic service. Eventually, husbands and wives working together made family agriculture a profitable enterprise for Japanese immigrants. Their farming success proved to be a bittersweet accomplishment, when long years later, the Japanese community endured loss of their land and incarceration during the Second World War.

In the nineteenth century, the larger society, with its intense anti-Asian feelings seldom distinguished between and among the various national groups immigrating to California. By the twentieth century, the Chinese and Japanese were lumped together as objects of hostility. This factor tended to keep all Asian women within their own communities and added to the invisible nature of their treatment in the historical record.

t night she dreamed the numbers: China 5 Exchange-4720, Lin Woo the cloth merchant; China 5 Exchange-2310, Woo Sung the manager of garden laborers; China 5 Exchange-1042, Bau Xi Wong the rice merchant. Her mother had taught her, making of the numbers and names a song with space for many verses so she would never forget.

It was the melody of her inheritance: a spot on the Chinese telephone exchange. The other girls would work in the laundry, or would stay at home, but she would take her mother's place at the switchboard in the beautiful three-tiered building constructed in the manner of a pagoda.

She liked to hear her mother talk about the first building, before it was destroyed by the earthquake: carved teakwood chairs inlaid with mother of pearl; the imitation Chinese oyster-shell window

panes, the lacquered tables; the ebony switchboard with gold-yellow carvings; the dragon that slithered in and out the plug holes.

Somedays they made a game of learning the numbers. While her mother was chopping vegetables, she would suddenly stop, turn to Li Li and say, "Lin Yoo, the herbal healer!" And Li Li would call out,

"China 5 Exchange-2134!" They would both laugh with delight, and her mother would hug her.

If Li Li spoke the wrong number, saying China 5 Exchange-5130 which was for Lin Soo, her mother would frown, shake her head and then sing, "Lin Yoo, the herbal healer, China 5 Exchange-2134," and Li Li would sing after her until she had embedded it anew in her mind.

Her mother would go about her work then, but after an hour or two, she would interrupt Li Li's play unexpectedly, shouting out, "Lin Yoo, the herbal healer!" And Li Li, without missing a bounce of the ball, would sing back, "Lin Yoo, the herbal healer, China 5 Exchange-2134," and Li Li's mother clapped her hands with joy and returned to the kitchen.

3

Indigenous Women

There were pioneer women who were not the pioneers. These were the women for whom the varied lands called "the West," had always been home. Native American women and Spanish speaking women, they watched the Anglo transformation of the land with a different, saddened eye. Tribe by tribe, group by group, they witnessed changes that touched their homes, their families, their own lives. They understood the word "invasion" in many forms, and they participated in the protection of land and kin. Their lives as women did not follow one common path. Clan and tribe shaped the experiences of Native American women, and these differed across the West.

After 1865, a series of wars, brought on by the increasing encroachments of whites and buttressed by Indians' earlier sour experiences with the U. S. government, thrust Native American women into the center of battle activity. Tribes moved hurriedly, sought refuge in hidden places, or whirled and faced pursuing troops. In these charged, chaotic events, Native American women seem only silent bystanders, as Anglo and Indian men played out the deadly clashes. Yet, this historical simplicity overlooks the place of women in native cultures, their varied roles, their powerful voices.

In the face of social, economic, and political upheaval, all Indian people struggled to maintain their tribal balance. For more than a quarter of a century, Indians across the West tried to negotiate a cultural resolution in a contest that pitted two differing systems against each other. Because the tribes left virtually no written records of their internal discussions, historians must extrapolate from external elements the apparent strategies of Indian people. That process has focused on male Indians— Cochise, Geronimo, Crazy Horse, Sitting Bull, Chief Joseph. These are the names highlighted in U. S. history. They are the figures pictured in the treaty discussions, the warriors in battle, the leaders in the reservation retreats.

Indian women appear only to have been the targets of soldiers' guns at such infamous locations as Sand Creek and the Washita. In the Anglo accounts of history, these women serve as the picturesque wailing mourners, mutilating themselves after the deaths of their husbands and sons, or standing silently as soldiers' horses swirl around in the aftermath of conflict. Some are remembered only in fading photographs from an Indian boarding school. Under the watchful eye of a superintendent or teacher, they stare out with somber expressions, their clothes carefully Anglicized, their hair trimmed or pinned.

But what of the ancestors to these young women? What of the weavers and potters whose artistry underwrote a tribal economy? What of the Indian women warriors, who went equally into battle? What of the women's guilds and societies? A woman's right to own and hand down her digging and tanning tools? What of marriage practices that allowed a woman independence of choice? Medical knowledge that kept young and old alive in a world closely connected to the outdoors? Divorce practices that

allowed a woman to end a marriage without censure? Women's councils that
decided issues of leadership and war?

Anglo society has overlooked diverse
economic, social, and political practices
within a variety of tribes. The place and
power of Indian women, misunderstood
by white soldiers, anthropologists, and
reformers, remain shrouded for those outside Native American cultures. Along
with that lack of information, outsiders
have also ignored the joy and laughter of
Indian women. Depicted only with
expressionless staring faces, Indian
women assume no character, no identity
for the modern white American. They
seem to be women without speech or
sound.

Yet, just the fringes of their history
reveal the folly of this view, for among
Native American people themselves the
names of women run like triumphant silver threads. The Apaches honor Lozen,
Victorio's sister, a woman who embraced
both the spiritual and physical processes
of resistance before her death in captivity
at Mobile, Alabama. Susannah Parker, by reason of adoption and
as mother of Quannah Parker, won her place among the Cheyenne. Sarah Winemucca desperately negotiated the slippery ter-
rain between the Indian and white diplomacy in an effort to halt
disastrous government policies imposed on the Paiutes.
Although at her early death from tuberculosis in 1891, Sarah
Winnemucca was granted scant eulogy from anyone, her life is a
monument to a woman who refused to be silent. Susanne La
Flesche, a Pawnee Indian, became the first Native American
woman physician. Despite criticism for some of her approaches,
she worked tirelessly to improve the health of Indian people,

often traveling long hours by horseback to bring medical care to small families. She was an ardent foe of alcohol use and envisioned the construction of a modern hospital to serve Indian people. Overwork and exhaustion contributed to her early death.

These women are among the few whose names, largely remembered through an oral history tradition, come to the modern world. In part, an enthusiast who wants names and accounts suffers from a misunderstanding of how native women achieved importance within their own cultures. Role and power did not necessarily demand "fame" in the traditional manner of Anglo history. Legitimacy for native women came out of established rights and expectations within their own culture, not from individual stardom so dear to most Americans. Somewhere in the history of the American West rests a rich and layered account of Indian women that waits to be reclaimed.

They will tell you that it is easy to diagram on a map: A B C D E F G H I. The Blackfeet. The Brule. The Cheyenne. The Minniconju. The Oglala. The Santee. The Sans Arc. The Two Kettle. The Uncpapa.

They will tell you there were six Arapaho. Captured because the others thought they were in league with the whites, later proven to be merely a hunting party.

Those are the Indians.

Easy, they will tell you: 1 2 3 4 5. Reno's advance. Reno's retreat to the trees. Reno's withdrawal across the river to the hilltop. Custer's stand above Deep Coulee. Custer's last stand against Crazy Horse, Gall, and Black Moon.

They will tell you that when Reno, a West Point graduate with Civil War experience, saw the enormity of the Indian encampment, he ordered his men to the cottonwood and the willow. They will tell you that the justification of that retreat has been disputed for over a century.

Maybe Reno was a coward. Maybe he was perfectly rational. Maybe he lost understanding or desire for any *war when a Sioux bullet spattered the brains of his scout, Bloody Knife, across his face.*

You will hear that Custer planned to strike from the north end of the camp at the same time Reno attacked from the south. You will hear that Reno did attack, fell back, retreated across the river to the hilltop. Custer was nowhere in sight.

And this was the battle:

Between five and six soldiers were killed running. The gray horses were mixed up with horses of different colors: the companies broke rank; they were confused and scattered. You will hear that the soldiers carried near-empty whiskey flasks. They will tell you about Lonesome Charley and about Lt. McIntosh, the mixed-blood. You will hear that Isaiah Dorman, the black interpreter, was tortured, shot in the legs, shot sixteen times with arrows through the chest and that a picket pin was rammed through his testicles. All this

because he was beloved by the Sioux. He had married a Santee, spoke Sioux fluently—and had turned traitor.

You will hear facts and gossip jumbled together: They will tell you about the lascivious habits of Colonel Benteen. That Benteen and Reno did not get along, that Custer and Reno did not get along, that Benteen and Custer did not get along. They will tell you how Custer, thirty-fourth in his class of thirty-four at West Point held the record for demerits: he grew his hair long, he rested with his feet out the window, he adorned his uniform. He may remind you, when you hear this, of your teenage sons or nephews.

He wanted adventure. He exuded the egotistical spirit of his culture; his hubris was accepted, even awarded. He literally kept rising, literally. In the spring of 1862, on orders, he climbed into a hot

air balloon to spy on Confederate forces near Richmond. Why didn't they pop his balloon? This vain man who later delighted in lashing his own men, this man who once dug a pit and is said to have ordered his own men into it for minor infractions of army regulations. They will tell you that Custer traveled with a sixteen piece band seated on white mounts, led by Felix Vinatiorri. They will tell you that Custer liked pretending to scalp his own men; that he lost 1200 men to desertion; that he witnessed an 8 percent suicide rate.

There are so many things to tell. What shall I tell first? What shall I leave until later? On June 25, 1876, Tashnamani was digging wild turnips with her friends a few miles from camp. Tashnamani—it means "moving robe." (Was it for the way her skirts swayed as she danced?)

The morning was sultry. The cottonwood were in full leaf and the stands of willow held an intense red. Tashnamani was twenty-three years old, still unmarried, still a virgin. She and her friends were chatting - about the men they hoped to marry, about the meal they would fix with the turnips. They spoke with respect about Sitting Bull.

From time to time, Tashnamani would stop digging and look around her. To the west she could see the nations' herds of horses. She remembered the song of Walking Elk greeting the rising sun. She could see the camp: hundreds of tipis. She sighed for the beauty of it.

When they had been digging a few hours, one of the women looked up to see a warrior riding toward them. The dust rising behind him brought to Tashnamani's mind a cloud of dust she had seen earlier rising behind a ridge in the east. The warrior was shouting. They waited for the breeze to carry the words to their ears.

Finally the sounds reached them: "Soldiers!! Soldiers!! Run to the hills with the children and the old ones!"

Tashnamani stood up, dropping her digging tool, an ash stick. It fell by the pile of gathered turnips. The others turned and ran; they called for her to come. The warrior was galloping back toward camp.

Tashnamani looked out at the land. This was one of her favorite valleys, thick with grass for the horses, covered with sunflowers. The river ran through deep clear pools. When the heat stifled her, the shadows of the trees were cool and dark. She looked at all of it. They had come here to rest, to regain spirit after last week's battle with these demons. They had come here to be a people on their own land.

She looked at her ash digging stick on the ground. The joy and hope she had felt earlier that morning was gone. She shook her head, as if to dispel a vision, and ran toward camp.

From her tipi, Tashnamani saw her father running toward the horses. In the next instant, she heard her mother keening, and turned to see her kneeling on the ground. She knew, at that moment, *that the mourning song was for her brother, killed by the soldiers. Turning from her mother toward the ridge, she saw the confusion on the rise just across Greasy Grass, the river the whites called Little Big Horn. She heard Hawk Man shout, "Hoke He! Hoke He!" And she watched the soldiers shooting and her father preparing for battle.*

Tashnamani began to sing. The death song for her brother rose to the air in tangle of grief and fury. Later she said. "My heart was bad. Revenge. Revenge."

When she finished singing, she painted her face crimson and braided her black hair. She ran to the thicket to take her horse. "I was not afraid," she said, "even though I was a woman."

Reno's men had formed a battle line. She could hear the carbines. Bullets shattered the tipi poles. Women and children ran back and forth in a snare of fear and anger. The old ones continued to sing the death songs. (Didn't the soldiers think this terrible keening was a war cry? And weren't they terribly wrong? Terribly ignorant?) Tashnamani remembered how she felt, "The enchanting death songs made me brave, although I was a woman."

She turned to her horse. A warrior dropped beside her, dead from a soldier's bullet. She and her father mounted their black horses and rode together to the stand of cottonwood and willow. They were joined by many others. Rain-in-the-Face cried out, "Behold! There is among us a young woman! Let no man hide behind her garment!" Rain-in-the-Face said of her that she held her brother's war staff over her head and leaned forward on her horse. He said she looked, "as beautiful as a bird."

Red Horse shouted, "There is never a better day to die." Tashnamani rode with him and the others through the powder smoke, her heart full of revenge. For the first time she killed a human being. One she shot; another she hacked to death with her sheath knife.

Tashnamani was not ignorant of battle. She had been on a raiding party, but this was different. This was destruction.

Much later, she would remember the beauty of the day before the attack. Like any of us would, she would remember that there had been beauty; and she would sift her memories of the knives and the guns and the screams of her kinsmen for visions of a glistening river, of fields of sunflowers, of myriad tents, and massive herds of horses.

But don't forget that the Battle of the Little Big Horn was carnage. Heads were found hanging from tent poles; bodies had been eviscerated, skin stripped, eyes gouged, skulls smashed. Soldiers who overran the deserted village in the days after the battle, cut the feet off Indian warriors or tore away their flesh to get at the beaded burial garments. Bodies lay naked in piles beside dead horses.

It is said that during the battle Tashnamani's friend, Tashnawambli (Eagle Robe) walked out from the village and pointed a revolver at one of Custer's interpreters, who had fallen wounded from his horse. He pleaded, "Please do not kill me, as I shall be dead in a short while anyway." And Tashnawambli answered, "If you did not want to be killed, why didn't you stay home and not come to attack us?" And having said these, the wisest words about war that anyone could say, and standing on the land the beauty of which was obscured by powder smoke, she shot him through the head.

The Blackfeet. The Brule. The Cheyenne. The Minneconjou. The Oglalla. The Santee. The Sans Arc. The Two Kettle. The Uncpapa. Reno's advance. Reno's fall back to the trees. Reno's retreat. Custer's stand above Deep Coulee. Custer's last stand against Crazy Horse, Gall, Black Moon.

These things are easy to see on a map.

But who can show me on a map the spot where the young woman, Tashnamani, dropped her digging tool of ash?

For women of Spanish-speaking families, the move into the West represented pointing the emigrant compass north. Many had arrived in the Anglos' "West" long years before any thought of an English presence. Some made their way out of Mexico and into the lands today called Texas, California, Colorado, Arizona, and New Mexico. From the arrival of the Spanish in the fifteenth and sixteenth centuries, a blending of the cultures of Spain and Native America began a new community of North Americans. For long years, persons outside the Spanish speaking communities of the West failed to understand the variations of culture among Hispanic groups.

In the 1880s, the migration of Mexicans into the United States exploded, adding to the numbers of Spanish-speaking persons already living in the Southwest. They arrived in an area where traditions of Anglo bias had been in place for long years and the economy for Spanish-speaking families increasingly depended on the work of all household members. In their general ignorance about the structure of Hispanic families, Anglos missed completely the role of women, whether married or single. A solid kinship system involved all family members in the support and care of the family. Though single women often took on the tasks of laundress or seamstress, the impact of their contribution was critical to the family's economic stability. Cultural outsiders overlooked the importance of women to the economic arrangements and dismissed Chicanas by virtue of the work they performed. They also failed to perceive that the woman's role as a wage earner outside the family evolved over time, so that one had to look closely at the current economic conditions for the Hispanic community in general to understand the work demands placed on women.

Once American business interests perceived the industrial potential of the Southwest, they saw the Mexican women as key players in helping to control immigrant male

workers. In an effort to "Americanize" the thousands of immigrants, companies set to the plan of trying to "educate" Mexican women to American middle-class values. Through classes in the domestic sciences, instruction from missionaries, and intrusion into child-rearing practices, the long arm of Anglo society reached into the center of Hispanic family life. The ultimate inability to "transform" Spanish speaking families into some version of the Anglo community speaks to the subtle and overt resistance especially exerted by Hispanic women, who sustained their own cultural values.

ynes Mexia was built like a finch: tiny, restless, quick. One day, when she was fifty-five, while she was collecting plant specimens at the top of a cliff in northern Mexico, she tripped. Her body catapulted off the cliff into the sultry afternoon air.

Built as she was, she seemed at first to fly, hesistating for a moment like a hummingbird, and then plummeting to earth.

In those moments, at once an instant and an eternity, she decided that if she lived, she would continue her work as a botanist.

What else is there? After you've known the flowers, and the mosses, the birds, the ferns, the palms, the herbs, the wild tobacco waiting in the field? When a woman can ride horseback in the Jaltepec, float in a dugout to Santa Lucrecia, wander through Peru, Bolivia, Argentina, and Chile, collecting a thousand specimens, stand above the Straits of Magellan, or amble through Mt. McKinley National Park in its early days, what would a polite education mean? Who or what would hold her back? Not age. She had no children—and her husbands were dead.

Living this life, her body knew its own sweat and ache, its strength, its fever, its weathered beauty. After all this, if a woman wanted, she could wear the skin of a rhea on her head when she gave a lecture and she could talk calmly, matter-of-factly about descending the Pongo de Manseriche on a balsa raft.

Mimosa Mexia was named for her. The genus of Compositae, Mexianthus Mexicanus, was given its alliterative christening to recall her and her service to the field of botany. Her advice on survival in the Andes was, it was said, invaluable to other scientists.

Perhaps you didn't know her before I told you this; but if you are a woman, you have known her all along. She is the prism of your dream; the light catches her in mid-air, and with a sudden intake of breath, you see the brilliant spectrum of your own colors.

4

Women of the Schoolhouse

*A*mericans recognize the schoolteacher as one of the standard female characters of the American West. Along with that recognition comes some fanciful imagery. Winslow Homer captured what Americans want to believe of the western teacher in his 1871 painting, "The Country School." Homer saw gentility and beauty in his teacher. His thoughts on the role of the teacher in the West reflect rather closely those of most Americans.

In the minds of Americans, a battalion of teachers, all young, single, beautiful, and white, marched into the West as the conduits of civilization. The western schoolteacher elicits a cherished and untainted memory for Americans; she represents one of the nation's historical heroines. Perhaps that affection stems from the fact that the young schoolteacher, who often married rather quickly, fulfilled two socially acceptable womanly roles—that of educator, followed by wife and mother. Regardless of how their historical reputation is explained, these women single-handedly embodied the conviction by a dominant culture that the values and lessons of its history should be transmitted to the children of the West. In fact, women did choose to journey from the East to the West for the express purpose of teaching school.

Often at the encouragement of the National Popular Education Board, young women, many of whom came from seemingly "sheltered" lives, took teacher training, signed two-year contracts, and set forth for unknown sites. In so doing, they reshaped the contours of their lives, enhanced the role of women as professional educators, and cut their own independent path as single women wage earners.

For some reason, Americans limit their view of the teacher to those women who worked in the elementary or one-room schoolhouse situations. Yet, it might be argued that in the West several different groups of women showed concern for education in varying forms. Directly and indirectly they influenced the growth of education within the West and about the West.

Parallel to the western schoolteacher, but largely ignored in the historical drama, was the frontier librarian. Although not strictly defined as teachers, librarians served as educators and promoters of learning in the American West. Their experiences and contributions to the institutional growth of the West make for another intriguing group of western women.

In the late nineteenth century, the trained librarian emerged as a new American professional. The West, with its scattered communities and culture-hungry citizens, represented a natural arena of interest for newly-minted graduates of library training programs. Spurred by local backers and, in some western locales, by money from the Andrew Carnegie library building fund, small communities sought to introduce permanent libraries staffed by trained librarians. These women, often the daughters of America's eastern middle class, came to the West for many of the same reasons as other single females. They sought employment, they hoped for the unusual, they felt a deep commitment to the purpose of library work as an agency of community reform and education. Almost without exception they faced a battery of challenges—poor facilities, inadequate funding, limited supplies, and cultural shallowness. Nonetheless, many of these women persevered, bringing to western residents regular access to literary works, timely lecture topics, matters of civics, and opportunities for citizen interaction. The women librarians especially welcomed women's groups devoted to book discussion and public debate. In burgeoning western towns, the library buildings themselves symbolized community and the women who staffed them, the advocates of civic growth.

Closely connected to the librarian was the woman of the West who took up the issues of women's rights and extension of the franchise. With their suffrage campaigns, lobbying expertise, and political results, these women deserve to be ranked as western educators. They worked for themselves, their daughters, other women, and ultimately, for American society at large.

Among the earliest of these crusaders in the West must be counted Abigail Scott Duniway, associated with the suffrage initiative in Oregon and Idaho. Duniway, who made the continental crossing on the overland trail and witnessed the death of her mother and brother, never knew a time in life when she did not perform grueling work for others. As a young schoolteacher in Oregon, following the death of her mother, she helped support her siblings. After a less than prosperous marriage, she struggled with a series of financial disasters that her husband wreaked upon the family. Finally, when he was permanently disabled in a work accident and Abigail took over the full management of the family, her spouse became convinced of the power of her drive and her commitment to women's suffrage. In 1871, she launched publication of a newspaper, the *New Northwest*, which she used as a pulpit from which to champion women's rights. Her public crusade took her through Oregon and into western Idaho. For a quarter of a century, she traveled the region in every sort of frontier conveyance and under miserable conditions to spread the message that the American legal system placed women at a distinct disadvantage. Her personality did not always meld easily with other suffrage leaders, either locally or nationally, but none would deny the forcefulness of her convictions. After years of bitter struggle, when Oregon implemented female suffrage in 1912, an elderly Abigail Scott Duniway registered as the first woman voter in the state.

Abigail Scott Duniway did not stand alone as a leader for women's rights in the West. In Wyoming, Esther Morris led the charge in a literal way. A large, outspoken woman, Esther Morris moved to Wyoming in 1869 and almost immediately emerged as an aggressive advocate for woman suffrage. Although other citizens may have had as much to do with the successful passage of the 1869 suffrage legislation, Morris became identified with women's rights. She served for a time as a highly effective justice of the peace and went to the national suffrage convention of 1895 as a Wyoming delegate. Her son, editor of the *Cheyenne Daily Leader*, may have somewhat inflated her reputation as a Wyoming reformer. Nonetheless, in 1960, Wyoming honored Esther Morris as one of its distinguished citizens by placing statues of her in Statuary Hall of the U. S. Capitol and before the Wyoming state house in Cheyenne.

As urban centers took more shape in the West, more and more women's clubs appeared. The Women's Christian Temperance Union, the General Federation of Women's Clubs, its counterpart the National Association of Colored Women, and the National Woman Suffrage Association all formed a wide umbrella under which women found legitimacy in organization. Although they engaged every possible subject from gardening to opera, formal clubs increasingly expanded the debate over women's rights. For example, the practical outcome of those discussions saw woman suffrage passed in Wyoming as early as 1869. Utah, long considered a bastion of conservative sentiment, followed with the vote for women in 1870. Although that action has often been dismissed as a Mormon church strategy to retain political control of the territory, women of the LDS relief society acquired a solid reputation for their progressive stance on issues related to female well-being. In 1895, feminists Susan B. Anthony and Dr. Anna Howard Shaw received a warm welcome from the Mormon women in Salt Lake City and posed for a historic photograph with such important leaders as Emmeline B. Wells and Zina Diantha Young.

In Colorado, women explored an alliance with state labor organizations that led to female suffrage in 1893. Utah's neighbor to the north, Idaho, produced its own complex grass-roots organization of local women, who saw the vote in place by 1896.

Throughout the West, in a variety of venues, women laid the foundations of community education and an extension of basic American political rights. Their efforts had a direct impact on their own lives, but also on the cultural traditions and expectations of western people.

PIONEER TEACHERS

*T*hey came for all the reasons Americans like to think they did. They answered a mission call, they responded to their own sense of responsibility, they wanted to be educators. In addition, they came because they needed to support themselves or send money home to aging parents or younger siblings. Above all, some came for the sense of independence and adventure that the West offered.

Unlike the pioneer wives and mothers, these women often traveled alone without the physical and financial security offered by a husband. Although they arrived with high expectations, women found the life of the pioneer schoolteacher arduous and frustrating, as well as liberating.

At the outset, the promised schoolhouse might be nonexistent or disappointing. Teachers often had to scour up the furniture and supplies themselves, serve as janitor, rid the classroom of snakes and bugs, haul water, protect the students from roaming animals, cowboys, or Indians, and teach all subjects to all grades. The challenge could be formidable and it was accompanied by low wages and a high cost of living. Some districts paid per head/per day, a system that lowered teacher salaries when children were absent for impassable travel conditions or seasonal farm and ranch responsibilities.

Teachers also struggled with loneliness. Unlike women surrounded by family members, teachers were usually drawn from the ranks of the unmarried and they came to the West alone. Their social opportunities closely monitored by contract regulations, teachers chafed under restraints that limited their every move. Off to school in the morning, home to the host family before dark, and a healthy dose of church activity framed the usual routine for the "schoolmarm." Even the latter could prove unsatisfactory when a young woman found herself working in a small community where the general religious persuasion differed from her own. Then, longstanding strife between Protestant denominations or across Catholic\Protestant lines could make life for the single, unmarried teacher nearly untenable.

Further, unmarried teachers suffered without family members to care about their well-being. The rigor of maintaining the school and teaching twenty different subjects to as many students often took its toll on a young woman. Each morning she faced alone a long day of physical and intellectual toil in a remote, drafty one-room schoolhouse, where discipline was a contest, when students ranged in age from five to twenty-two.

When these difficult routines wore away a young woman's emotional and physical reserves, illness assumed more dangerous tones than it needed. Too often a young woman, without a watchful eye from attentive family, neglected her health or failed to seek medical care. The combination of obstacles—social restrictions, poor pay, community bias, physical hardship, broken health—sent some women back to the East after the fulfillment of the two year contract.

Despite the various drawbacks for the teacher, the western experience offered many positive lures for those with a taste for challenge. Women who left the East uncertain of their skills and themselves often built an inner confidence they never expected to develop. Others discovered the fun and adventure that had eluded them in the East. Still others, whether they remained in the West or returned to their homes, made happy matches and retired from teaching. Local girls, often still in their teens and with only an eighth grade education found a source of professional employment with a promise of upward mobility.

Working with limited resources in small communities, teachers reached inside themselves for teaching inspiration and creativity, revealing their deep commitment to the professionalization of American education. They seized on opportunities to further their own education or to advance to an administrator's rank. Collectively, the teachers enlarged the positive image that Americans held of women educators and the importance of schooling. Overall, the group of western teachers contributed to the growing sense among nineteenth-century women that their gender could succeed and accomplish, while doing work essential to the advancement of the community.

he records report that she was thin and frail and suffered from asthma, was five feet and two inches tall, with large blue eyes and very dark hair. It is written that she was teaching school in Wisconsin when she met George Frary, and that she married him at age nineteen and came West when he decided to move to Denver. You can read that in Denver, she bore four children: Edgar, Guy, Grace, and Lottie; and that in 1889, the family moved to Salt Lake City, because George loved it. The record shows that two years later, the family moved to Antelope Island, just four miles north of the ranch that is surrounded by green trees and covered by blue sky. You will hear that there were three more children: Dora, Frank, and Florence.

And though the records report that Alice Phillips Frary was an exceptional teacher, you will hear little else until the story of her death on 3 September 1897.

I want to bring back the woman that lived those six years on this island. I don't believe she lived those years as a frail, asthmatic woman, whose only life was a mouselike concern for her husband and children.

She asked to be buried on Antelope Island, and I think she asked this because she was a woman of passion for the world, because it was on this island that "she had known moments of wonder, had slipped out of the boundaries of the ordinary and gathered mysterious moments to herself, like a miracle come down to her for breakfast."

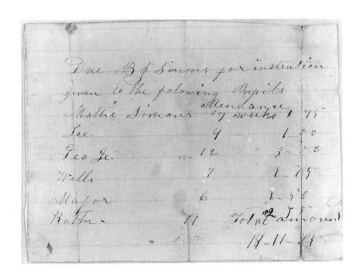

No one else knew about her secrets, but I do; and I will tell you some of them:

She had never been to Guatemala, but every May, when she woke, she thought about it. Particularly when she was out hanging the laundry.

Pinning up one of her husband's shirts, she would look up to see curlews flying over, toward the beach. They moved without effort on the air currents, and as she watched them, she could feel her spirit lift and escape from her body that yes, was too often shaken and rattled by asthma.

During those spring days, she watched the curlews mate, nest, and lay eggs; and when the young were big enough in June, she watched them head south, to Guatemala.

Alice gave this—and all her secrets to her children. She gave them the curlews, the forty fresh springs on the island, the Farmington Canyon rocks (2.7 billion years old); she gave them the bobcats, and the muledeer, the willits, eared grebs, and all the owls: long- and

short-eared, barn owls, great horned owls swooping low over their heads, covering the land with their shadow. She gave them the plum trees in the orchard, the tender purple drawba in the early spring, and the sound of coyotes in the early morning hours. She gave them snakes: garter, gopher, and racers. She gave them gullys of maple and chokecherry, meadow and horn larks, and brilliant beetles, hobbling through the cheat grass. She gave them sandpipers and sand fleas on the north end of the island, and a vision of snow on the Oquirrhs.

She knew other secrets; she knew stories.

One day in early spring, she told them the story of Annie Barlow, who had ridden on one of the newly broken wild horses on an outing with a group of friends. "That horse just remembered its freedom," Alice said, looking straight into the eyes of her children. "It remembered its freedom, and how it felt to run loose and feel the wind against its hide, and it just wheeled away from the rest of them, up, up into the hills, jumping from crag to crag, and the others screamed and cried. They thought Annie was lost for good. But the horse just needed to be free for a little bit, and when it had enough, it carried Annie right back to the ranch."

Another night, in the middle of winter, when her children were all sitting with her by the fire and the wind was pushing at the corners of the cabin, she told her children how in 1884, the men of the Island Improvement Company had shot all the wild horses left on the island, so they could bring in Hereford and Galloway cattle. After she told her children this, she closed her eyes and sat silently. The children could feel the wind slap the windows. They shuddered—and they wondered, each of them, what a herd of wild horses looked like, and they wished they could have seen such a thing as that. They thought about the herd of elk, killed by vandals just that year—1894. They kept silence like their mother.

In February 1893, Alice showed them the stuff to make their own stories. She took her children to wait for their father and the Walkers and their men, to watch them bring the buffalo to the island by boat. Standing on the southern shore, they watched the boat with its high makeshift sides slide and tilt toward them. Inside, the two old bulls,

Alexander and Napoleon, battled each other, hurling their giant carcasses against the frail wooden sides of the craft.

These were all Alice's secrets. And the biggest one was that she looked and saw: to ask to be buried in a place means that you love it; that it is a place that allows you to "slip out of the ordinary and gather the moments of wonder."

In early fall, 1897, Alice Frary fell ill. Her husband, affectionately called Bumma, sailed in his sloop, the "Water Lily of Tooele" across the lake to Syracuse, then rode horseback to Ogden for medicine. Returning to Syracuse, he saw three fires burning on the eastern shore of Antelope Island. He recognized the sign for distress.

It is said that not long after her death, Alice's four-year-old son, Frank, turned up missing one winter day. Hours later, his older brother spotted his cap bouncing up and down with the gait of his walk through a herd of buffalo on the south side of the hill. The older boy was afraid he would cause a stampede if he called or ran to his younger brother. He watched while the bright cap appeared and disappeared in the mass of hide and hooves. When Frank ambled up to the gate, his brother hugged him close and asked, "What were doing, Frankie? Where have you been?"

The little one, who had walked the eight miles to the ranch and back in the snow, blurted out, "I went to get my two good mittens."

His mother had envisioned a wild pony remembering its freedom. She had created for them the sight of buffalo coming to the island, she had dreamed the curlews on their long journey. She had dreamed a world where people were at home in this beauty, an island where her children could bound from rock to rock, certain of their journeys.

ROMAN CATHOLIC TEACHERS

*I*n the saga of the West, this group of pioneer educators is commonly overlooked. Often at the request of a western bishop, Roman Catholic sisters (commonly called "nuns"), set forth for remote mission stations from Kansas to California, from Montana to Texas. Present in the West from some of the earliest days, sisters, especially German and Irish immigrants, increasingly moved into the region after the Civil War. Although the sisters seem to have been few in number during the "frontier days" of a community, in actuality several thousand of the professed religious lived west of the Mississippi River by 1890. They represented a number of different orders, some with European origins, some American founded. Their ranks included the Daughters of Charity, the Franciscans, Benedictines, Dominicans, and various branches of these orders.

Most mission groups consisted of four to six sisters, usually selected by a mother superior for a western assignment. Like their secular counterparts, sisters traveled under extreme hardship to remote, new communities only to discover the promised residence and school more illusionary than real. Often treated with great kindness by strangers, Catholic and non-Catholic alike, sisters still encountered some very direct religious bias. Undaunted, they lived in church basements, abandoned buildings, and private homes until a small convent could be constructed. They supported themselves and expanded their missions through the charity of the town and their own ingenuity.

Almost every mission superior begged the motherhouse to send a music teacher, for such a sister nearly singlehandedly kept the convent operating on money earned from giving piano and violin lessons. The local pastor also gave support, although this source could prove unreliable, as other church demands made the sisters last on the list for parish funds. In addition, pastors often expected sisters to take on cleaning services for the church or rectory as a requirement for the monthly stipend, a request that led to vigorous debate between some priests and those mother superiors who refused to add more domestic work to the sisters' already overtaxed mission schedules.

Typically recruited from the East to launch a small academy for girls, sisters often shifted their original plans to meet the needs of a community. Although residents might have requested a school, the absence of a medical facility or the presence of several orphans often forced the sisters to expand the scope of their operation. Thus, Catholic schools, hospitals, orphanages, and community centers began to dot the American West.

By the 1880s, more young women born in the West and taught by mission nuns began to seek admission to convents. Convent life, in addition to its spiritual attractions, offered the opportunity for personal advancement and the chance to become a teacher. Even those assigned primarily to convent domestic work also taught their cooking, sewing, and fancy work skills to pupils.

Perhaps most appealing was the fact that western convent life, despite its traditional emphasis on cloister, brought nuns into direct contact with interesting persons and differing cultures. Mother Caroline of the School Sisters of Notre Dame crossed paths with Tom Thumb. Brigham Young, leader of the Mormons in Utah, developed an agreeable relationship with the Sisters of the Holy Cross in Salt Lake City. The Franciscan Sisters of Glenn Riddle, Pennsylvania, spent their Sundays cooking and serving hot meals to groups of Indians who came to their small Kansas mission.

However, only a few Native American women, despite their exposure to Catholic education, gravitated toward convent life. For example, early in the twentieth century, two native students from the small parish at Windthorst, Kansas, entered the Sisters Adorers of the Most Precious Blood.

Perhaps the greatest boost to western Catholic education came from Mother Katharine Drexel, foundress of the Philadelphia-based Sisters of the Blessed Sacrament for Indians and Colored People. Mother Katharine, who inherited millions of dollars from her father, underwrote the western endeavors of a variety of religious communities before she established her own order of nuns. Her money supported reservation schools in most western states, including Kansas, Montana, Arizona, and New Mexico.

Long convinced of her own religious vocation, Mother Katharine, after many difficulties, launched her own community in the early 1890s. A shrewd businesswoman and an able administrator, she invested her vast fortune in the cause of education for children of color. After 1890, she continued to provide financial assistance to other religious orders, but concentrated on building missions and schools for the Sisters of the Blessed Sacrament. She traveled extensively throughout the West, always insisting on the importance of education for Indian children.

Her first Blessed Sacrament mission, a project for which she assumed complete planning and construction oversight, opened in 1902 at St. Michael's, near Gallup, New Mexico. At St. Michael's, as well as other mission schools, language barriers

and cultural differences caused Indian parents pause about the desirability of Catholic education for their children. Later in life, some Indian graduates retained mixed feelings about their boarding school experiences, but most acknowledged the order and dedication of the sisters in the mission field.

The presumed constraints associated with convents and the cultural clashes paramount between native and Christian religions have tilted Catholic western history into a gray zone. Yet, from a woman's perspective, the West introduced dramatic and challenging times for women, as religious people and as educators.

UNIVERSITY PROFESSORS

*T*he West ranks as that region of the country that first opened the doors of the public university to women. For example, women entered the University of Minnesota in 1851. In the next few years, other institutions fell into line, so that by 1870 women had access to the classrooms of at least eight different western states. In all of these places, special regulations restricted most aspects of a woman's education. Nonetheless, the accessibility of advanced curriculum meant that women enjoyed unprecedented opportunities to explore the world of higher education in the West. The knowledge that females could secure a university degree in the West sent a message to all American women, and in the closing years of the nineteenth century, colleges felt the pressure to admit a new and eager constituency.

As important as these classroom experiences were, they should not completely block from view the experiences of the woman scholar. Often overlooked in a discussion of "schoolteachers," these women, who reached out for the highest intellectual achievement, made research and educational contributions to all Americans. For example, botanist Alice Eastwood began her academic career in 1879 as a teacher in Colorado. An assiduous student, she turned her attention to the botany of the Rocky Mountains. Within a few years, scientists everywhere recognized her as the leading expert, not only in plants,

but in the regional geography and geology as well. She extended her study of botany beyond the Rocky Mountain area, collecting and cataloguing thousands of specimens, as she acquired an international reputation for her far reaching scientific knowledge. She held the position of curator of botany at the California Academy of Sciences for almost sixty years and stands as a legend among academic women of the West.

For some, the university offered teaching opportunities, for others a research atmosphere or a chance to advance into administration. All helped to advance the women in American education within the West and beyond.

xcited by love for her fiancé, Katherine would think in the names of plants and flowers. On the day the two of them began their wedding walk from San Diego to San Francisco, just as they were walking along a cliff above Mission Bay, with the ocean churning over the rocks below them, she was thinking "solidago," goldenrod, known, among many other things, as an aphrodisiac. As soon as it came to mind, she blushed and turned her face away toward the sea.

Her husband took hold of her chin and gently turned her face back to him. "Why are you blushing?" he asked.

"Solidago." She answered.

He laughed aloud and took her hand.

They walked along, the forty-five-year-old doctor, blushing from her own passion, and her new husband, a forty-seven-year-old civil engineer, laughing for joy at her side. The sea breeze cuffed their faces and tousled her hair and his; their rucksacks rested easily on their backs. Botany was their common language. The beauty, healing powers, the surprises of plants encoded in names, spoke for them.

Ambling along, she remembered her youth: her nine rambunctious brothers; her father, the "impractical genius"; her dark mother, of the iron will. On this particular day, she wanted to tell her new husband about all of them: the reckless childhood games, the fiesty dinnertime conversation, and the outdoor curiosities.

"My mother and father encouraged us," she smiled at her husband, "they raised me like the boys."

"Ah, you may have the energy of a boy, but you're certainly not a boy!"

"Now, you're blushing!" She laughed.

She felt intensely whole as she walked along beside him. She tread an earth she recognized: she could name the rocks, the plants, the trees; she could feel the wind, the sunshine, the rain, and, she was in love.

"We moved west from Tennessee, lived one year in Salt Lake City, then packed up and took the train to California. We would have gone on, but the ocean stopped us."

He reached over and mussed her hair.

"Then I grew up, taught school, and married the Irishman."

"When you tell me this, you always call him 'the Irishman'? Why not 'My first husband'"?

"Because even though I was sad when he died, I felt released. I used to spend my free moments watching birds and studying insects. He never liked any of that. He didn't dislike it either. He was oddly neutral toward the world; he was a man I didn't know. And all the time I was fantasizing about being a doctor." She hesistated. "And about walking along the ocean with a man of passion."

The storekeeper in Oceanside asked them their name. They smiled at each other, "Oh, we're the Burdocks." It was a joke, but the storekeeper didn't get it.

Katherine apologized. "Please forgive us. We were being silly. Burdock is the tramp of the plant world, and we're walking along like tramps."

The storekeeper's face was blank. The two thanked him and hurried out.

That night after they made love in their camp on the beach, and he was breathing deeply in sleep beside her and the waves had settled in their rhythm, the names of plants and flowers swirled through her mind. Since she had studied materia medica, *and made her choice of botany, the names filled her head:* Circaea quadrisulcata, enchanter's nightshade, for the plant Kirke used to drug the men of Odysseus. (She had only to think it, and she could imagine how she could charm this new husband.) She thought "emetic": Y. breifolia, the fruit of the Joshua tree; she thought "yucca leaves" and knew how to cure headache. She envisioned mothers in labor and thought "wild tea" so the babies would slip out the women's dark bodies into the world as easily as fish leap into the air above a lake, and she thought "laceration" and could see herself crushing to a spongy mass the fresh-scrubbed roots of the yarrow. She let her mind slide over the four flowing sounds of fragaria and knew how she would bathe her husband's eyes with this juice of the wild strawberry when he was tired or how she would make tea of it when he felt a cold coming on. She thought "blue—like his eyes, or this sky, or this sea," and she could in an instant see the lupines that she loved most: bluer and paler than periwinkle, bluer than zenith, a blue that could be food.

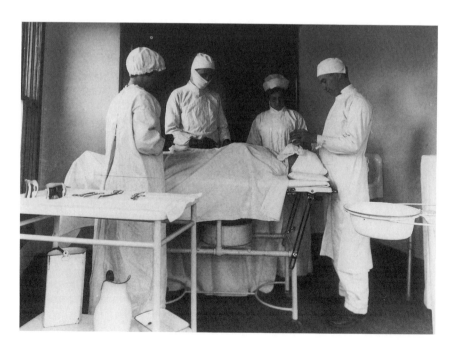

Katherine knew this walk would end; there had been many end-ings in her life. They would go back to work. They would have argu-ments; they would get old. But for this moment, in this darkness, she let the sound of the sea, the gentle fatigue in her legs, the odor of her husband's skin mixed with salt air, and the names of the plants rush through her mind. And when she finally slept, with her arm thrown across her husband's chest, just before dawn, she dreamed of a child who had been born without the ability to laugh. In the dream, she mixed solidago canadensis *with water and the bone of a squirrel that had died at the same time of the child's birth, and she washed him in this mixture.*

This, she had learned, was what the Meskawkis knew—each plant a history and pharmacy in itself.

5

Women of the Criminal World

Nowhere in the scenario of western womanhood does one find the woman criminal. References to prostitutes—the petty criminals of everyone's society—abound in the West, yet a fully-developed definition of criminal women seems somehow out of place in the American West. What laws, after all, would they have broken? Where and how, in the masculine West would they have been punished?

Women criminals comprised an element of western woman-hood. Some women compiled a long list of arrests for minor crimes. They, like Lottie Stotts of Austin, Texas, accumulated numerous charges for vagrancy, drunk and disorderly conduct, public brawling. These women made regular appearances in the local justice-of-the-peace courts and helped to keep the city coffers filled with a constant supply of small fines. When they could not pay the fines and court costs, they languished in the local jail for about thirty days. Usually well known in small western communities, these women became the regular targets of local newspaper reporters, who generally treated them with unmitigated contempt. Mocking articles, larded with phrases such as "the fallen ones," "a hideous excuse for a woman," "strumpets," "things calling themselves women," made those who broke the law into objects for public scorn.

When their criminal actions spilled over into the area of violent felonies, then these local "fallen women" found themselves on the short end of compassion and justice. Hastily assembled trials were remarkable for their lack of balance and intemperate assessment of guilt in the public press. Trials ended quickly with swift convictions and stern sentences. Once convicted, these women, especially those of color, were no longer held in the local jail, but were hustled off to the state penitentiary.

Sometimes women's criminality involved the deliberate attempt to break the law. For example, in 1902, Pearl and Gertie Smith apparently got themselves involved with a pair of male thieves who went from store to store in Cheyenne, Wyoming. While the women distracted the clerks, the men hoisted as much merchandise as possible. Other women, like "Mormon Kate," turned to typical "female" crimes—forgery and embezzlement— to sustain themselves. Of course, women did commit violent crimes. Often these resulted from long periods of physical abuse, which prompted women to strike back at brothel customers or husbands. However, the nineteenth-century legal system had little place for self-defense pleas from abused women. A conviction for manslaughter or murder, regardless of the circumstances, usually meant a woman faced a minimum sentence of twenty-five years in prison.

More women in the West fell out with the justice system than has been acknowledged in history. Poor women and women of color lived under an uneasy truce with the law and its enforcers. If charged with a crime, such women faced almost insurmountable odds in the courts. They relied on court appointed attorneys, of whom only a few argued aggressively on the client's behalf.

Few persons in the community appeared willing to cooperate with the defense, and the newspapers indulged in sensational trials by press. If convicted, a woman risked severe penalties, especially when compared to men who committed comparable crimes. In part, this stemmed from a social inclination to punish women more for violations of gender codes than for commission of crimes. For women, guilt and innocence remained less important to the western judicial system than the rupture in the expectations of womanly behavior.

Accordingly, women faced their prison time without much hope of early release or parole. Women of color usually served a full sentence, as did white women who were repeat offenders. In Texas, Arkansas, and Missouri, middle-class white women who committed major crimes often received a full pardon, while still confined to the local jail. Their families had the ability to hire the best known lawyers, men with the necessary political connections to the governor's office and parole board. In this manner, white women of greater economic resources could secure special consideration from the state. Regardless of class, all women who collided with the law encountered a cold and foreboding system, for a perceived disregard for the woman's code of conduct evoked a stern response from society. In the West, where the jails and prisons rarely conformed to basic standards of human decency, women paid an extreme price for any type of criminal violation.

PROSTITUTES

*I*n American film, no western barroom scene would be complete without the presence of the dance hall girl. Cloaked in mystery and myth, this denizen of the saloons has been the glamorous accoutrement of Western movies and novels for over a hundred years. In the storybook presentation of the saloon

woman, one finds only beauty, youth, and the tragedy of a
wasted life.

   According to moral prescriptions, dance hall girls or prostitutes filled an important need in western bachelor communities.
After all, for lonely, single men of an "untamed" West, the presence of the beautiful prostitute offered some tarnished distraction
from homesickness and an "acceptable" outlet for physical needs.
Still, no one really could fully condone the prostitute's "life of
sin," so American audiences, who have learned all they know of
these western women from a variety of slick films and television
shows, have always expected to see some form of social punishment for the fallen woman. Destined always to be a moral outcast,
perhaps she died at the hands of some crazed cowboy, or lost the
hand of her true love, who left the saloon to marry the lovely, vir-
tuous schoolteacher.

   As with many of our images of women in the American West,
this one is flawed. Since it suggests an easy explanation for the

existence of deviant women and offers just a splash of sexual decoration, the concept of the beautiful but pathetic prostitute has lingered in the American imagination.

Actually, prostitutes lived out a difficult life with many forms of social, economic, and political constraint. The ranks of the West's poor and the uneducated supplied the prostitutes for the region's boom era of the nineteenth century. Women entered the profession at an early age—twelve- or thirteen-year-old prostitutes were not uncommon. In 1877, a Denver woman, Mrs. Whatley was reported to have been overseeing her fifteen-year-old daughter's life of prostitution for at least three years. Cheyenne prostitute Ella Harvelle abandoned her two younger children in a local brothel, while her fifteen-year-old daughter went off to live with yet a third madam.

Rather than single women on their own in the world, prostitutes frequently married and raised children. Their husbands not only knew about their employment, but expected them to continue to work on a regular basis to augment family income. Prostitutes, with or without husbands, often cared for several children and moved their families from one brothel to another. Many of the women could not read or write and had few opportunities to extricate themselves from their lives by entering better types of occupations.

Prostitution did not readily lead to a life of ease. Women drew their clients from among their own socioeconomic circle, and typically these men did not have great amounts of money to spend on women. Further, there is little evidence to indicate that men wanted to reward women generously for sexual services. On most occasions, both parties negotiated the price under conditions of mutual suspicion and confusion. The woman bargained for the best price and then tried to get more, while the man aimed for the opposite. Disagreements over the payment of fees led to thievery in the brothels and physical fights between prostitutes and customers. Angry, well-liquored clients who awakened to find a wallet or a gold watch missing did not hesitate to attack prostitutes with knives, guns, and fists.

In addition, women dealt with high overhead expenses on a daily basis. City officials often levied a regular "tax" against a madam and she paid if she wanted her operation to remain open. Madams also showered officials with gifts to keep the arrangements cordial. In Boise, Idaho, madam Agnes Bush sent the police chief a diamond badge through the local Elks lodge. In Denver, in the 1870s, the larger bordellos—the Corn Exchange, the Cricket, and the Occidental Hall—avoided the annoying fines and arrests endured by some of the lesser-known saloons, presumably because the owners had bought their way into privilege with local officials.

Beyond the politics played by the wealthier members of the vice community, individual women had to pay off pimps, hack drivers, and hotel clerks. Landlords charged them exorbitant rents. Sheriffs and marshals expected personal gifts and favors. Court costs and lawyers' fees further drained limited resources. In the long run, the opportunity to make a sizeable profit and to successfully save or invest it, occurred for only a few of the thousands of prostitutes working in the American West.

Even those who managed to accumulate some wealth found that the basic conditions of the life touched all. Violence, both imposed and self-inflicted, created an unsettled atmosphere in their lives. The prevalence of alcohol and drugs further imperiled the women. Prostitutes felt the full force of customers' wrath, intentional and accidental. Sometimes the violence was directed at the women themselves. In Austin, Texas, in a two year period, eight different men were brought before the court on charges of assaulting prostitutes. In 1879, Edward Malone nearly throttled to death Cheyenne prostitute Ida Snow, before another customer mortally wounded the attacker. On other occasions, a hapless young woman simply got in the way during a brawl between two customers. A black prostitute, Georgie Cox, died when she stepped between an irate customer and the madam who operated a brothel outside of Fort Russell in Wyoming.

106 N. Main St.

Yoounito.

In this cycle of poor wages, unattractive working conditions, and widespread violence, it is not surprising that prostitutes died at young ages. Some died from the results of long term abuse of their health, malnutrition, tuberculosis, or alcoholism. Others died from mismanaged abortions, murder, or suicide. All in all, the image of the western prostitute as a carefree, highly sophisticated beauty overlooks many of the social and economic realities of the nineteenth-century West.

These realities have not deterred some municipalities from advertising their prostitutes and madams as historical tourist attractions. For example, the madams of Denver—Mattie Silks, Laura Evans, and Jennie Rogers—acquired colorful reputations in the folk history of the city. Each, prominent in her day, seemed to affirm the notion that women could earn a handsome wage and enjoy glamorous adventures in prostitution. Yet, each lived under the same constraints of public discrimination, police harassment, and professional uncertainty as the less famous among the demi-monde. The same threat of sudden chaos and personal violence filtered into their worlds. Regardless of whether a woman worked inside a fancy brothel, sought customers as a street walker, solicited from rough cribs in back alleys, or camped outside frontier military garrisons certain difficult conditions circumscribed the essence of her life. Perhaps the mistake has been to measure prostitutes' lives only by the apparent material goods they acquired and not by those elements that touched the quality of their daily existence.

Manuela dreamed. It was always the same dream and it went like this: She was living with her children in the mountains of New Mexico. One son was the son she had, the other child was the girl she had aborted, come back to her womb, born, and grown to be five years old. The children's father was living with them in the cabin; but in the dream he was a shadow at the corner of the house, a movement in her peripheral vision that she could not capture.

In Manuela's dream it was summer, and the children were playing on the hillside above the lake. Manuela would step out onto the board porch and at that instant, both children would look up from their digging and run to her across the rocky slope, shouting, "Mamma! Mamma!"

She would watch them scurrying the pebbles in their path and would descend to meet and gather them in her arms. They would press their faces into her stomach, wrapping their arms around her legs.

In the dream, Manuela could feel their hands, chests and faces through her dress and she hugged them close, grasping their cheeks in her hands, kissing their eyes and smooth foreheads, holding their looks with her own so they could see the love in her eyes.

She gathered every detail of their onyx hair, their tawny skins, their bright teeth, and she willed with her look for them to carry her love with them.

"Do you want to walk down to the lake?" She asked in this dream. And in this dream, they shouted in unison, "Yes!"

Without turning back to close the door, she strode off toward the trail to the lake. And in the dream, she could hear them chattering, behind her, and in the dream, she could see the lake below the rock cliff from where, on a moonlite night, she had hurtled herself through the sultry air into the cool water.

The guard slapped her hard across the face. He was pouring beer over her. "Bitch," He spat the word at her. "When I'm pokin' a woman, I want her to pay attention."

This was one of the mean ones.

Maybe I am wrong. Maybe that was not her dream. Maybe this was her dream:

Manuela knew a nun named Sister Katerina. Sister Katerina lived with five other nuns in an adobe house behind the church. Manuela thought these five women were the most beautiful women, besides her mother, that she had ever known; and Sister Katerina was the most beautiful of all of them. The sisters spoke in gentle but determined voices, and they knew how to read and write in Spanish and in Latin. Some of them knew English as well.

Manuela's dream went like this. When she was old enough and the day came that she was to leave, she walked to the river carrying her small basket of clothes. After she had washed her skirt and two blouses, she and her mother pressed and packed them neatly.

When Sister Katerina came to the door, Manuela turned and kissed her mother goodbye and walked to the wagon with the sister, who sat beside her in silence all the way to the convent, where Manuela was to become a postulant.

The girl struggled to contain her excitement. She would be educated, she would be a nun, and she would work for her own people, and especially, she would find girls like herself, whose passions were for education.

The man ran his hands roughly down the length of her body. "Filthy bitch!" He spat the words at her. "When I'm doing my business with a woman, I expect her to pay attention."

This was one of the mean ones.

No? Well, maybe third time is a charm. Manuela had a dream. It was always the same one. In her dream, Manuela was neither a wife, nor mother, nor nun. She was a curandera. *From the time she was six, she roamed the desert and the river bank with her grandmother, gathering plants. Her grandmother taught her all names and the meaning of the names: wild rose and mint for relaxation and sleep, chokecherry twigs simmered in water for fever, the wild geranium for astringent.*

As she learned to gather, her grandmother taught her as well how to prepare the herbs. Stinging nettle would increase a mother's milk. Wild tea from yucca was to ease the pain of childbirth. Disregarding the nettles, Manuela's grandmother folded the dry plant in her hands, wrapped it in a scarf along with a small package of the tea and sent the girl to Señora Estevez who was in childbirth. Manuela watched the woman twist in the pain of labor. Over the earthen stove, she prepared the pudding of nettle and the broth of yucca. After the woman had drunk the broth, Manuela stared at her face: a band of sweat broke out on Señora Estevez's forehead, and Manuela saw her muscles relax.

When her grandmother came after an hour, Manuela rushed to the end of the bed so she could see the baby rush out: a bloody mass that in an instant grew legs and arms and a head with a mouth that squealed. Manuela watched it all. She was certain her plants had done this. Her plant had created a child out of this oozy pulp. She told her grandmother this, but the older woman only laughed and hugged her. "No, Manuela, no. Our plants only ease the mama's pain. Only G-d creates, He tells us which plants to pick; you and I are just His farmers. That's a good thing, don't you think? To be G-d's farmer?"

Manuela nodded. She felt relieved. She prefered small but important work. It seemed to fit in her hands.

After the night of Señora Estevez's confinement, Manuela left the house of her mother and went to live with her grandmother. She wanted to sleep there, with the plants drying on the rafters above her. She wanted to rise early and walk in the dawn desert with the old woman. She wanted to learn how one leaf could turn away such an evil thing as sickness. How the bitter herb, boiled and cooled could ease the enemy of pain.

The man pinched her at the waist. "Hey, whore!" He spat the words at her. "I want my women to pay attention."
He was one of the mean ones.

Manuela was twenty-one when she entered the Arizona territorial prison in Yuma. Her son, whom she was never to see again, was eight years old. He was living in a Catholic orphanage with nuns who loved him, in their strict way, but none of them, he noticed every time they came close, smelled like his mother.
Manuela had been convicted, with her pimp, of murder. It was the pimp who had killed the man—for money—but he had been let off, and Manuela had been incarcerated. A fifty-year sentence, with seventy-five men as cell mates.

Do I have the courage to tell you this? Do you have the courage to hear it? After all, Manuela was a prostitute. What difference, then, did it make?

She started as a child. I can see her black braids bouncing against her back as she runs through the village. She is being chased by her brother in a game of tag, and they are laughing. As they get older, her brother not only chases her; he catches her—and not for tag. And she is not laughing.

Do you wish I would not say this? Do you wish I would just be quiet about it and not mention these things? I am sorry.
Her brother raped her when she was twelve, and the child of that union was her son, who went to live with the nuns.

There are things I have to tell, whether I want to or not. A man overpowered a woman, and she had nothing to say about it, and this happens too often.

Manuela stayed in the village. When her brother had used her enough and the word got round, she became a prostitute. What else was she going to do under such derision? No one would have her for a decent wife. She learned to swear, she learned to lie, she learned to harden her heart, she learned to steal from the pockets of the men who were using her, even as they did it.

She was not innocent in the murder. She wished them all dead. One by one as they mounted her, she wished all these dogs dead. So, when her pimp slit the man's throat, she was not sad.

Manuela was a prostitute, incarcerated in the Arizona territorial prison with seventy-five men. The warden of the prison, it is said, knowingly allowed the men to use her for sexual purposes, and no one knows what happened to her.

No one knows what dreams she dreamed, and no one knows if she loved her son.

INCARCERATED WOMEN

Little or no provisions were made for incarcerated women in the West, whether confined to local jails or to state and territorial penitentiaries. Although Americans tend to think that women seldom, if ever, went to prison, a steady stream of women entered various penal institutions across the West.

Typically, women arrested for minor offenses—prostitution, drunkenness, disorderly conduct—served short terms in local jails. Their cases were heard in the justice-of-the-peace court, and their terms were usually not longer than thirty days with a fine for court costs.

However, more often than realized, women served their time in state prisons built for and staffed by men. Within these confines, women served hard time. Authorities made little or no housing or work arrangements for women and allowed their care to slip into a morass of physical and sexual abuse. Medical attention was particularly shoddy and most women, if they survived, left the penitentiary in broken health.

For many years, matrons were unheard of and male guards had the power to dispense generous doses of physical punishment, much of which bordered on the barbaric. The wooden horse, the bat, and various chain devices were used in western penitentiaries until well into the twentieth century. In addition, women

spent time in the dark hole on bread and water for minor infractions, or commonly, if they were discovered to have become pregnant while in the prison.

When authorities did devise some work for women, it tended to focus on domestic skills. Women cooked for the institution, cleaned the warden's quarters, and made clothing for the male prisoners. If the state contracted prison labor out to a private businessman, the domestic work of women took on "sweatshop" conditions. For example, in the early twentieth century, the women prisoners at the Missouri penitentiary, made shirts and pants for a private company. They started the day with a skimpy breakfast and worked for ten to twelve hours at antiquated sewing machines. The windows of the workroom were painted over, the only ventilation provided by a few old fans trained on the supervising matron.

Few women prisoners left written records of their experiences. This helped to expunge their penitentiary time from the public consciousness. For this reason, the letters of a well-educated prisoner, like Kate Richards O'Hare, offer special insights into penitentiary conditions for women. O'Hare served time in the Missouri state penitentiary for anti-war activities during World War One. As a political prisoner, along with the famous Emma Goldman, O'Hare actually enjoyed a number of niceties not available to other women. For example, she had ready access to the warden, received many food gifts from family, and had another prisoner clean her cell. Despite these amenities, O'Hare proved a keen observer of the penitentiary routines and her descriptions detailed the hardship faced by all females, within the western penitentiaries.

Black and Hispanic women entered western penitentiaries in numbers disproportionate to their totals in the surrounding community. For petty thieveries and other minor offense, women of color received sentences that ranged from two to five years at hard labor. In contrast, often authorities confined white women to the

local jail or pardoned them before they entered the penitentiary. Thus, racism fueled the penal system of the West and added to the general uneven equality that ethnic people experienced.

When any woman went to a western penitentiary, she stepped into a world of brutality, one which made small accommodation for the care of female prisoners. In addition, a general societal indifference to the fate of such women created an atmosphere that made their lives seem unimportant, both in their own time and in the historical record. Nonetheless, their stories form a portion of the western experience of women.

6

Women of the Fort and the City

WOMEN OF THE MILITARY

*A*mong these would be some women who traveled to the West with the U. S. army. Wives of officers and enlisted personnel shared in an aspect of western living distinctly different from many other women. Often young and ill-informed about the West, typically a recent bride, these women found themselves thrust into some of the most rural locations, where they lived under taxing conditions. Because the forts gave visual and unrelenting affirmation to the many tensions between white and Native American cultures, a mood of uncertainty and insecurity prevailed for all. Military women, few in number, lived each day unsure of the surrounding world and ill at ease within the masculine army community.

The military caste system did not encourage casual mingling between officers and enlisted soldiers, and that code carried over to women's social relationships. An officer's wife often hired her

cook, servant, or cleaning woman from among the wives of the
enlisted personnel, but the two were not free to pursue a peer
friendship. Most officers' wives came from white, eastern middle-
class families, so differences in social status and education
helped codify the hierarchy, as did the presence of a number of
African American women among the domestic group.

The wives of enlisted men and the camp followers, in addition to employment with officers' families, worked as laundresses, a military support unit provided for in army regulations.
Considerable variation existed in the personal lives of these
"suds row" residents, usually assigned to the most rudimentary
huts and tents for quarters. Some lived in traditional marriages

with soldiers, but others were single, often traveling with several small children. Among both the married and the single laundresses, prostitution provided a way to supplement slim earnings and meager rations.

Officers' wives looked for more "acceptable" activities to fill their time. They sponsored a range of fort social events, promoted literature and music, and often conducted Sunday school for the children. Many passed the days by keeping detailed journals, in which they recorded vast amounts of topographical and cultural information. As a result, Americans read about the West from the personal writings of a Frances Roe, *Army Letters from an Officer's Wife, 1871-1888* or an Emily McCorkle Fitzgerald, *An Army Doctor's Wife on the Frontier: Letters from Alaska and the Far West, 1874-1878*. Other military wives looked back and collected their memories into publishable form. Martha Summerhayes with *Vanished Arizona: Recollections of the Army Life of a New England Woman*, Mrs. Orsemus B. Boyd with *Cavalry Life in Tent and Field*, and the prolific Elizabeth B. Custer with a series of books left fascinating, if sanitized, accounts of the frontier world of military women. In these combined ways, military women took on the role of voluntary educator.

More than other Anglo women, army wives came into contact with Native American women. These contacts covered a range of experience, but most were tempered by the Protestant sensibilities and ideas of "civilization" of the military women. Nonetheless, the army wives often served as the conduit for educating those white Americans who had little or no interaction with native peoples. For example, Mary H. Eastman encountered the Sioux Indians around Fort Snelling, Minnesota, in 1841. Driven by her own desire for a literary career, Eastman acquired some knowledge of the language and recorded first hand accounts of the Sioux way of life. Her own sense of womanhood colored her understanding of Indian gender dynamics and prompted her to write critically of Sioux women. Despite the narrowness of the perspective that permeated her work, Eastman drew attention to Indian life and to the experiences of Native American women.

Military women probably did not fully appreciate the uniqueness of their opportunity for interaction with Native American women. So many different factors—fear, compassion, interest, distaste, language, friendship, racism—swirled through the contacts that it must have been difficult for women from either society to decipher exactly what resulted. A special moment in women's history passed—and left modern society with only a partial record of its dynamic.

URBAN WORKING WOMEN

*T*hey came to the new cities of the West for the same reasons that men did—they wanted work. They took on any venture. For all, survival and a chance to profit from the booming western economy directed their energies.

Women worked as seamstresses and milliners. Washing and ironing kept many a woman employed, and if her own business faltered, she could attach to a local military regiment as a laundress. In Denver, Hannah S. Hutchinson secured temporary employment as an enumerator for the 1880 U. S. census. She lived in a local hotel and earned other income selling hygienic undergarments.

Women worked as clerks in legal offices. They managed restaurants and sweated in bakeries. They secured jobs as reporters for city papers. They became professional photographers. They went to work for city governments. Telephone companies employed them as operators. Women found positions with dress shops and drygoods stores. They nursed the sick in the new hospitals of the West. They sorted olives in California. They did fancy needle work in New Mexico. They handled freight in Wyoming.

In each of these urban worlds, industry and economic development surged upward through the nineteenth century. Along with that financial growth came an ever increasing demand for women

as workers. In the West, the emergence of cities meant more and
more women employed in the public work-force.

7

Work, Grief, and Joy

The commitment to a life grounded in the land and its elements brought western women an unexpected boon. While
women may have known about the standards of ladylikeness and
Victorian decorum, the realities of the West often demanded
something quite different. The exigencies of farming, the presence of large animals, the requirements for survival drove women
into an intense relationship with the outdoors. Almost without
their realization, western women emerged as a new physical type
within the sphere of femininity. Accomplished, toughened, and
confident, women accepted any physical task or regional trial.
They not only managed the climate, they strengthened themselves through their constant handling of large animals. Horses,
cattle, oxen became their companions. Once assigned only to care
for chickens and hogs, women in the West branched out to the

demands of bigger livestock. They learned to herd bawling steers across rushing streams, rope horses, and brand cattle.

Though women probably gave it little thought, the work demands of the West forced them out of doors to a healthier life in the invigorating fresh air. The fragile image of women, cultivated in eastern society, fell away in the West. While respiratory ailments, especially tuberculosis stalked the East, western women and their daughters acquired a robust vigor that helped curtail the much feared "wasting diseases."

As the outdoors became a natural arena for women, their attention turned from just the chores of that world to its pleasures. Western women increasingly took up the physical world as a place of enjoyment. Their skills included snowshoeing through wintery mountains, marksmanship, and every trick associated with cattle and horses. Although Americans seemed to believe that only a single eastern-born celebrity, Annie Oakley of the Buffalo Bill Cody Wild West Shows, was comfortable with horses and guns, many western women honed such skills. The recreational activities of ordinary western women foretold of a later time, when Americans would herald the female athlete.

As their pleasure in the western landscape increased, so did their concern for understanding and preserving it. Even a transplanted easterner, such as the botanist Jeanne Carr, could learn to appreciate the magnificence of the West's natural world. In 1869, her adventuresome spirit impelled her to visit the giant redwoods and Yosemite Valley. Shortly after, she scaled a highly dangerous section of the Sierra Mountains. Overwhelmed by the beauty of these encounters with nature, she encouraged her long-time friend, John Muir, to take the cause of conservation to a public forum.

Other women aggressively engaged the West, as well. In the 1860s, Martha Maxwell moved to Colorado, where an accidental meeting with a taxidermist furthered her already strong interest in the creatures of the natural world. By the 1870s, she was recognized as an exceptional naturalist, who observed animals and birds in their habitats, hunted them herself, and then tried to recreate the natural environment in her taxidermy exhibits. By the

time of her early death in 1881, she was acclaimed across the
nation for her work with western wildlife.

As western women passed beyond the earliest stages of migration into the West, their self-confidence and personal expectations grew. The first newcomers carried their cultural and
emotional baggage of other lives in other regions into an
unknown world. Those who followed them or were born in the
West reaped the benefits. They learned from the letters and
accounts about the hazards to be avoided and the precautions to
be taken. These later women faced the West with less trepidation
and more anticipation for the adventure and opportunity it suggested. As a result, the story of western women is not unilateral.
Rather, it takes on the hues of differing time periods and the tex-
ture of many personal perspectives.

*T*have always imagined her stepping onto the train in Buffalo as a woman and stepping off in St. Louis as a man. That must be the way she did it. A desperate, determined woman could bring it off.

She was born in 1847, the daughter of wealthy Irish parents, part of the Buffalo aristocracy. Bearing an illegitimate child as a teenager must have been a trauma to both her and her family. I try to imagine her, full of desire and womanhood, on the night her son was conceived. She would have worn a green velvet ball gown, and would have been dancing with the man she loved, oblivious to the possibility that he would jilt her, or that her parents could shun her, or that within a year she would be living in a New York boarding house on the lower East Side trying to support herself and her baby by working as a kitchen maid.

The baby was healthy, a boy. She named him Laddie. Though she supported him the rest of her life, she never saw him after she made her strange and fascinating choice.

I try to imagine her trip West. In the train station in Akron, Ohio, she would have stepped off the women's car with her satchel, entered the darkened hallway at the far side of the station room, and ducked into the men's room. There she would have frantically pulled out the trousers and rough shirt from her bag, dug out the scissors tucked in the bottom; she would have chopped off her hair, bound her breasts with the cloth wrap she had packed, tugged on her boots, and crammed on her head a floppy brimmed hat that obscured her pure complexion and hairless face. She could have done this. Then walked back out to the platform, turning not to the steps of the women's car, but to the men's. She could have sat in a corner in the men's car, jamming her head even deeper into the hat, and trembling with the audacity of what she done, fallen into a fitful sleep.

At Independence, she could have signed on with a Mormon wagon train, driving cattle to Zion. And they could have been good to this young boy, who knew nothing of horses or cattle, who seemed so delicate that he might not last the trip. And on the train, it is possible that one day, along the Platte, the top hand, Dan, could have discovered Little Joe, rising out of a secluded spot in the river after a bath, and understood at that moment of beauty, why he

had been troubled and disturbed by this boy for all the weeks since he had joined up with them.

And it could be that by the time the train reached the cutoff south of Fort Hall, Dan, who had kept Little Joe's secret and had taught her how to handle horses and cattle and a gun, was also ready to ask her to marry him.

And it could be that she refused because the earlier pain had been too much and because at night when she slept, she still could hear Laddie crying for her. So it could be that she said goodbye. And for certain, she rode into Idaho City, one day in the spring of 1867, and someone commented, "Now there's a sprightly Irish lad."

How young she was, with womanhood a secret, to begin thirty years as a lonely man. In the solitude of the Idaho mountains she learned to rope and shoot, to wrangle sheep, to sheer. By the time she came out, surely she must have toughened, her skin tanned and cracked.

She moved to Silver City, in the Owyhees, to mine. From there, discouraged by a "trusted partner" who stole her savings of nearly $3000, she drifted to Malheur County in eastern Oregon where she worked as a hired hand until 1880. She had saved enough to home-stead a ranch on Succor Creek.

Little Joe was determined to support her son in the way she imag-ined best: by being a man, by beating at his own game the fiance who had been a traitor to her. She became a better man than he was. She was quiet, honest, hard-working. She rode better than the other cowboys at that border of Idaho and Oregon, slept outdoors in all seasons, never complained, out-shot anyone around. She served on jury duty and voted conscientiously. For a brief time she was a movie star. All this, and she paid child support regularly.

I try to imagine her: a short, stout, fifty-six-year-old woman, whose child was only a dream, whose womanhood must have become, with the years, a fantasy of the dark, after-dinner hours in her dugout when the Chinese hired-hand had left for the day.

After she died, everyone claimed to know who she was. After she died. A New York Post *article said that, as a man, Little Joe had graduated from Columbia Law School and had been admitted to the New York State Bar. The* Lewiston Morning Tribune *in Idaho said she was "none other than Kate Bender, the notorious Kansas murderess..."*

Late in December of 1903, Little Joe started out with her herd toward winter pasture on the Boise River. She had been ill. By the time she reached the Malloy Ranch, a few miles east, she was too weak to go on. Mrs. Malloy took her in and nursed her as much as Little Joe would allow, but the first week of the New Year, sitting in a chair in the front room, Little Joe died of pneumonia. The circumstances of the discovery that Little Joe was a woman are understandable. Yet it is painful still to know that it was two men who discovered her secret.

THE GIRL CHILD

*R*egardless to which family or ethnic group she was born, her life had a prescribed path. No girl child of the West would miss out on the work. Although all children worked within all cultures, custom usually dictated that boys' daily chores had an ending hour, after which lads were free for recreation. Girls' work tended to overlap into both male and female spheres, allowing for few breaks in the daily schedule, and consuming most of the waking hours. Work stood as the defining feature of the gender.

From her earliest days, when still at play, a girl learned the patterns of work expected within her culture. That four-year-old walking with family to a distant western homestead might skip and hum, but she would be scooping up buffalo dung for the evening fire as she went. Hunting for hidden objects trained little Indian girls to be alert for the berries they must start to find by the age of six or seven. Chinese girls took an early place beside their mothers in the family business. They learned about restaurant work, or the family store, or the Chinese theater. Milking the family cow thrust a six-year-old farm girl into the center of the family economics and responsible for a task that could never be skipped for games. Requiring a five year old black child to stir the boiling tub of wash got her ready for that day when she might take in laundry to keep her own family supported.

Food gathering, child care, cooking, garden tending, laundry, house cleaning— all were woven into the fabric of play for girls from every culture. In only a short time, certainly by the age of ten, the play and the work mix began to separate. The games became less frequent, the structure of chores more fixed. Work, the constant companion of women, shaded the future of the girl child.

THE BRIDE

*A*ll the cultures had brides. With the exception of the Roman Catholic nun who had no interest in acquiring a spouse, most of the women of the West expected to marry and raise families. Some married by choice, some by family arrangement, some in great joy, some with deep sorrow. Across these cultures, these races, these classes of women, each understood the realities of marriage that they faced. As surely as elegant, beautifully gowned young women joined hands with fresh-faced West Point graduates, so did migrant prostitutes bond with merry barkeeps in the eternal search for happy matrimony. Young Indian women accepted gifts of ponies and young Asian women searched a crowded room for the face that matched the photograph supplied by the marriage

broker. Hispanic women, in the center of family, walked to the altars of small mission churches. Mormon women, surrounded by sister wives, entered into contracts little understood by those beyond the Utah borders. European immigrant women stood next to strange men they had only read of in letters and repeated vows in marriages arranged by families. Some married out in the great rural spaces of the West, others in raw urban towns. Some followed sacred ritual, others sought a justice of the peace.

For each of these women, whatever the atmosphere, the moment changed her existence. She moved from "girl" to "wife." With that change, dramatic in itself, came additional pressures wrought by the cultural upheavals of a place called the American West. Her own expectations, her own hopes for marriage succeeded or faltered often because of social and economic forces in the West that overcame the personal plans of individual couples. The West, itself, became a third partner in the marriages of people from all cultures. For some couples the West symbolized the meaning of opportunity, while others watched this same process and felt only loss for themselves and the children they would have.

Each woman, in the face of these powerful regional forces, needed to become an advocate of her spouse, a protector of her family, and an activist for her own culture. Too often, each of those elements carried with it personal pain and unreasonable sacrifice. In assuming all these roles, along with their accompanying personal pressures, women, as individuals, have blurred in the historical memory.

Yet, within each culture of the West, women, as wives and mothers, carried forward banners of strength and cultural identity. More often than not, within their cultures, they depended on each other for courage and support. In the most difficult environments, in the most trying times, they developed their own networks, their own language of survival. Because of the edifying,

singular history left by each generation, the daughters who followed them could continue to add to the heritage of western women.

UNIFYING ELEMENTS

*A*cross cultures, women were not the same. They spoke different languages, worshipped different gods, laughed at different jokes. They often did not know each other and did not want to. Bitterness and hostility frequently marked the interaction of their various cultures.

Their commonalities are not so obvious. An immigrant homesteader lived much as a black one did, but always with better resources and never with the same fears of a violent explosion of racism. A Chinese woman in the center of San Francisco Chinatown hardly replicated the life of an Apache woman struggling with her band to escape the noose of the U. S. army.

Even the women we thought we knew from the West—the pioneer wife and mother, the schoolteacher, and the dance hall girl—prove not so easy to know. Their lives involved motives and circumstances that we have covered with a slick veneer. They offer as many differing stories as there were women.

They did share, even as they felt they did not. They shared within their sense of womanhood the keen experiences brought by great happiness and great sorrow. It is through their understanding of the nature of happiness and tragedy that they form

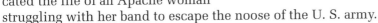

their unbreakable bonds across cultures to each other. The joys
and the griefs that enveloped western women transcended cultural boundaries and brought together as one the common women
of the American West. All women exalted at the first cry of a new-
born child, all wept at the last death rattle of a beloved. Each had
her day when she rocked with mirth at a funny song, a coarse
joke, a silly sight. Each lowered
her head in sorrow from a cruel
blow, a hungry family, a painful
insult. The linchpin of a universal bonding rested in the aspira-
tions that women held for their
families and their relatives.
Above all, they held dear to a
common love for their children
and a desperate hope that the
future West would be an easier
one for their kin. The tragedy of
the American West may well be
that women of all cultures never
came together in the unity of
laughter and tears. In their own
eras, many women of all cultures
resisted acknowledging the reality of their melding, denied the
sameness of motherhood, the
parallels of gender. In the recognition of this universal truth—
that all women, despite their
uncommon lives, are bound
together in the commonality of
womanhood—are found the
threads of unity for modern
women of every class and race.

*T*he baby Emma Wetherhill succumbed to cholera at a campsite on the Platte River. Her mother and father were British immigrants, newly converted to the Mormon Church, and they were bound for Utah.

When Emma died, Catherine Wetherill clasped the baby to her breast and refused to give her up. There was a wild, "Stay away from me" look in her eyes.

It took her husband, David, more than an hour to convince her they would have to bury the baby. "Not bury, David," she cried out. "Not bury. The animals will dig her up."

David watched while she bathed the small body and swaddled it in white strips of cloth torn from her petticoat. When she was finished, she handed the corpse to him: "Not in the ground."

Heavy with his own grief, he stood beside the wagon holding his sad burden and wondered what to do with it.

One of the hands, Joe, came up with the answer. "I heard the Apaches sometimes hang their dead in the trees so no animals will get to them. Do you want me to take little Emma and do the same?"

David Wetherill nodded.

Joe mounted his bay and accepted the bundle. Without looking into his friend's eyes, he reined to and rode off toward a stand of cottonwood downriver, where a stream joined the Platte. At a sturdy willow that stood next to a giant cottonwood, he dismounted, took off his vest, and fashioned a sling for the tiny corpse. Then he picked his way up the willow and leaned over to secure the bundle to the thick limb of the cottonwood. He used strips of the same white petticoat in which the baby was swaddled; making a kind of swing, so that when he let go, the baby rocked gently as a cornflower in the breeze.

Joe climbed down, turned once to look back at the child swinging lazily in the pure air, mounted his horse, and rode back to the wagon train.

The next morning, Azuma Hooks rode out to bring in the remuda. By the time the sun broke the lip of the horizon, the train was on its way. Catherine Wetherill sat in the back of the family wagon watching the campsite recede. She squinted to see the stand of cottonwood. The grove of trees was barely visible, but she *thought she detected a flicker of white against the dark of the limbs.*

She was not crying. Her grief was not liquid; it was packed in her heart, tight and explosive as shot. She was in a struggle with this grief and she had to gather all her strength. She had to ignore everything around her: children, husband, the dust, her backache from the jarring of the wagon; her hair hanging in dirty strands around her face. She had to ignore the ocean of prairie, the sand in her

rough boots, the grit in her teeth. She had to efface the pieces of plank with the names of children burned into them that she had seen too often along the trail. She had to ignore the angry fights she had heard among the emigrants, the accusations, the petty competitions for a place near the fire or for a bed in the wagon.

At this moment, she had to think only of the baby. She squinted hard at the distant clump of cottonwood.

When they had gone just a mile, David heard Catherine cry out, "I've got to go back."

Before he could rein in the team and set the brake, Catherine had jumped from the wagon and was running back toward the grove of cottonwood. David leaped down and ran to stop her; but Joe, who had been riding along beside the wagon and had heard everything, called out.

"David, it's all right, let me take her."

He reined his horse toward the direction from which they had come and urging it to a trot, rode up beside the fleeing woman. She stopped and turned her face up to him. She wasn't crying. She was determined.

"Will you come with me, Catherine?"

She nodded and let him pull her up onto the saddle behind him.

In the shade of the tall trees, the sunlight dappled their clothes and faces. Beneath the burial tree, she stood close to Joe.

"I just felt I had to be with the baby. Just be here." Catherine spoke without raising her head.

"Do you want me to check and make sure the ties are secure?" Joe asked.

Catherine nodded.

Joe climbed into the tree and reached toward the strips of cloth that suspended the baby's body. The bundle wiggled. Joe groaned, as if someone had punched him. He glanced down at Catherine and then back at the bundle. It wiggled again.

"Is it secure?" Catherine was looking up at him.

"I'm going to retie the strips just to make sure."

Joe undid the knots and lifted the bundle into his arms. It was wiggling. He started to unwrap the baby.

"Stop Joe! I didn't mean ..."

"No, Catherine. Emma's wiggling. She's alive."

Suggested Readings

A broad and rich literature focuses on women in the American West. Just as this book is only an introduction to some of the themes that touch women's western lives, this list represents only a small portion of the many available works. It is also intended that these sources would be readily accessible to the general reading public. The items here should lead the interested reader to many other readings.

Apostol, Jane. "Jeanne Carr: One Woman and Sunshine." *American West.* 15 (July/August 1978).

Arnold, Abraham. "The New Jerusalem: Jewish Pioneers on the Prairies." *Beaver* 74 (August–September 1994).

Armitage, Susan and Elizabeth Jameson. *The Women's West.* Norman: University of Oklahoma Press, 1987.

Azuma, Eiichiro. "A History of Oregon's Issei: 1880–1952." *Oregon Historical Quarterly* 94 (Winter 1993–94).

Boyer, Ruth McDonald, and Narcissus Duffy Gayton. *Apache Mothers and Daughters; Four Generations of a Family.* Norman: University of Oklahoma, 1992.

Butler, Anne M. *Daughters of Joy, Sisters of Misery: Prostitutes in the American West*, 1865–1890. Urbana: University of Illinois Press, 1985.

———. "Women in Prisons of the American West, 1865–1920." *Western Legal History* (Fall\Winter 1994).

———. "Still in Chains: Black Women in Western Penitentaries, 1865–1915." *Western Historical Quarterly.* (February 1989).

Chinn, Thomas W. *Bridging the Pacific: San Francisco Chinatown and Its People.* San Francisco: Chinese Historical Society of America, 1989.

Chittenden, Elizabeth F. "By No Means Excluding Women." *American West.* 12 (March 1975).

Cordier, Mary Hurlbut. *Schoolwomen of the Prairies and Plains: Personal Narratives from Iowa, Kansas, and Nebraska, 1860s to 1920s.* Albuquerque: University of New Mexico Press, 1992.

Deutsch, Sarah. *No Separate Refuge: Culture, Class, and Gender on an Anglo-Hispanic Frontier in the American Southwest, 1880-1940.* New York: Oxford University Press, 1987.

Dick, Everett. *The Sod–House Frontier: 1854–1890.* Lincoln: University of Nebraska Press, 1937, reprint ed., 1954.

Escobar, Corrine. "Here to Stay: The Mexican Identity of Moapa Valley, Nevada." *Nevada Historical Society Quarterly* 36 (Summer 1993).

Fletcher, Maurine S. "Alice Eastwood: A Scientific Adventurer." *American West* 17 (January/February 1980).

Godfrey, Kenneth W., Audrey M. Godfrey, and Jill Mulvay Derr. *Women's Voices: An Untold History of the Latter–day Saints, 1830–1900.* Salt Lake City: Deseret Book, 1982.

Goldman, Marion S. *Gold Diggers and Silver Miners: Prostitution and Social Life on the Comstock Lode.* Ann Arbor: University of Michigan Press, 1981.

Gray, John S. "The Story of Mrs. Picotter–Galpin, a Sioux Heroine." *Montana: the Magazine of Western History* 36 (Spring 1986): Part One; (Summer 1986): Part Two.

Gutiérrez, Ramón. "Honor Ideology, Marriage Negotiation, and Class–Gender Domination in New Mexico, 1690–1846." *Latin American Perspectives* 12 (Winter 1985).

Harris, Katherine. *Long Vistas: Women and Families on Colorado Homesteads.* Niwot: University Press of Colorado, 1993.

Helfman, Bill. "'Sun Rising in an Eastern Sky': Japanese Americans in Washington Township, 1920–1942," *California History* 73 (Spring 1994).

Herr, Pamela. "School Days on the Frontier." *American West* 25 (September/October 1978).

Jordan, Teresa. *Cowgirls: Women of the American West, An Oral History*. Garden City: Doubleday, 1984.

Kaufman, Polly Welts. *Women Teachers on the Frontier*. New Haven: Yale University Press, 1984.

LeCompte, Mary Lou. *Cowgirls of the Rodeo: Pioneer Professional Athletes*. Urbana: University of Illinois Press, 1993.

Leckie, Shirley A. *Elizabeth Bacon Custer and the Making of a Myth*. Norman: University of Oklahoma Press, 1993.

de Léon, Arnoldo. *They Called Them Greasers: Anglo Attitudes toward Mexicans in Texas, 1821-1900*. Austin: University of Texas Press, 1983.

———. *The Tejano Community, 1836-1900*. Albuquerque: University of New Mexico Press, 1982.

Maret, Elizabeth. *Women of the Range: Women's Roles in the Texas Beef Cattle Industry*. College Station: Texas A&M University Press, 1993.

Mazel, David, ed. *Mountaineering Women: Stories by Early Climbers*. College Station: Texas A&M University Press, 1994.

McBroome, Delores Nason. *Parallel Communities: African Americans in California's East Bay, 1850–1963*. New York: Garland Publishing, 1993.

Moore, Jesse T., Jr., "Seeking a New Life: Blacks in Post–Civil War Colorado," *Journal of Negro History* 78 (Summer 1993).

Myres, Sandra. *Westering Women*. Albuquerque, University of New Mexico Press, 1984.

Peavy, Linda, and Ursula Smith. *Women in Waiting in the Westward Movement: Life on the Home Frontier*. Norman: University of Oklahoma Press, 1994.

Petrik, Paula. *No Step Backward: Women and Family on the Rocky Mountain Frontier*. Helena: Montana Historical Society Press, 1987.

Poling–Kempes, Lesley. *The Harvey Girls: Women Who Opened the West.* New York: Paragon House, 1989.

Riley, Glenda. *Frontierswomen: The Iowa Experience.* Ames: Iowa State University Press, 1981.

––––––. *Women and Indians on the Frontier, 1825–1915.* Albuquerque: University of New Mexico Press, 1984.

––––––. *The Female Frontier: A Comparative View of Women on the Prairie and the Plains.* Lawrence: University Press of Kansas, 1988.

––––––. *A Place to Grow: Women in the American West.* Arlington Heights: Harlan Davidson Press, 1992.

––––––. *The Life and Legacy of Annie Oakley.* Norman: University of Oklahoma Press, 1994.

Rothschild, Mary, and Pamela Claire Hronek. *Doing What the Day Brought: An Oral History of Arizona Women.* Tucson: University of Arizona Press, 1992.

Schultz, Elizabeth. "Dreams Deferred: The Personal Narratives of Four Black Kansans." *American Studies* 34 (Fall 1993).

Stewart, Kenneth L., and Arnoldo de Léon. *Not Room Enough: Mexicans, Anglos, and Socio–economic Change in Texas, 1850– 1900.* Albuquerque: University of New Mexico Press, 1993.

Stockell, H. Henrietta. *Women of the Apache Nation.* Reno: University of Nevada Press, 1991.

St. Pierre, Mark. *Madonna Swan: A Lakota Woman's Story.* Norman: University of Oklahoma Press, 1992.

Tamura, Linda. "Railroads, Stumps, and Sawmills: Japanese Settlers of the Hood River Valley." *Oregon Historical Quarterly* 94 (Winter 1993–94).

Terrell, John Upton, and Donna M. Terrell. *Indian Women of the Western Morning: Their Life in Early America.* Garden City: Doubleday, Anchor Books, 1976.

Tong, Benson. *Unsubmissive Women: Chinese Prostitutes in Nineteenth Century San Francisco.* Norman: University of Oklahoma Press, 1994.

Sources for the Stories

Angier, Bradford, with illustrations by Arthur J. Anderson. *A Field Guide to Medicinal Wild Plants.* Harrisburg, PA: Stackpole Books, 1978.

Barton, William Eleazar. *Old Plantation Hymns: A collection of hitherto unpublished melodies of the slave and the freedman, with historical and descriptive notes* New York: Ams Press, 1899.

Chinn, Thomas W. *Bridging the Pacific: San Francisco Chinatown and Its People.* San Francisco: Chinese Historical Society of America, 1989.

Connell, Evan S. *Son of the Morning Star: Custer and the Little Bighorn.* New York: Harper & Row, 1984.

Dodge, Bertha S. *Plants That Changed the World.* Boston: Little, Brown, 1959.

Hardorff, Richard G., comp. and ed. *Lakota Recollections of the Custer Fight: New Sources of Indian-Military History.* Spokane: Arthur H. Clark, 1991.

Idaho State Archives, Boise, Idaho.

James, Edward T., Janet Wilson James, and Paul S. Boyer. *Notable American Women, A Biographical Dictionary,* 3 vols. Cambridge: Belknap Press of Harvard University Press, 1971.

Marshall, William H. *The Major English Romantic Poets.* New York: Washington Square Press, 1963.

Parkman, Francis. *The Oregon Trail*, ed. E. N. Feltskot. Lincoln: University of Nebraska Press, 1994.

Sanders, Jack. *Hedgemaids and Fairy Candles: The Lives and Lore of North American Wildflowers.* Camden, ME: Ragged Mountain Press, 1993.

Sanders, Scott R. *Wilderness Plots: Tales About the Settlement of the American Land.* Columbus: Ohio State University Press, 1973. See p.

115-17. The idea of a list of the ways people died comes from this book by Scott Sanders.

Siporin, Louis, and Sally Karmelenski. Oral interviews by author, 20 December 1994. Omaha, NE.

Photo Credits

1. "Madonna of the Prairie," 1921, William Henry David Koerner, oil on canvas. Courtesy of the Buffalo Bill Historical Center, Cody, Wyoming.

2. "The Homesteaders," 1932, William Henry David Koerner, oil on canvas. Courtesy of the Buffalo Bill Historical Center, Cody, Wyoming.

3. Unidentified Utah woman, ca. 1913. Courtesy of Special Collections and Archives, Utah State University, Logan, Utah.

4. Unidentified graves. Courtesy of Steve Siporin.

5. Dugout on the South Loup River. By S. D. Butcher. Solomon D. Butcher Collection. Courtesy of Nebraska State Historical Society, Lincoln, Nebraska.

6. Shack covered with tar paper. First home of Charlotte T. Theall, Keoma, Alberta, Canada, 1911. Courtesy of Milton T. Theall, Weston, Massachusetts.

7. Charlotte T. Theall at her home in Calgary, ca. 1912. Courtesy of Milton T. Theall, Weston, Massachusetts.

8. Page of sheet music for "The Colorado Trail."

9. A gathering of Native Americans in Indian Territory, possibly including descendants of African Americans. Hudson Collection. Courtesy of the Western History Collections, University of Oklahoma Library, Norman, Oklahoma.

10. Page of sheet music. "Before I'd Be a Slave."

11. Homestead of an African American family near Gutherie, Oklahoma Territory, 1889. Swearingen Collection. Courtesy of the Western History Collections, University of Oklahoma Library, Norman, Oklahoma.

12. The Shores, a family of musicians homesteading near Westerville, Nebraska. Solomon D. Butcher Collection. Courtesy of the Nebraska State Historical Society, Lincoln, Nebraska.

13. Ada Blayney, Oelrichs, South Dakota, ca. 1909. Courtesy of the Nebraska State Historical Society, Lincoln, Nebraska.

14. Nancy Hendrickson planting corn, Morton County, North Dakota, ca. 1918. Courtesy of State Archives and Historical Research Library, State Historical Society of North Dakota, North Dakota Heritage Center, Bismarck, North Dakota.

15. Spring plowing on the Stasney farm, a few miles south of Mandan, North Dakota, April 23, 1906. By Brown Land Company. Courtesy of State Archives and Historical Research Library, State Historical Society of North Dakota, North Dakota Heritage Center, Bismarck, North Dakota.

16. Chinese women working in San Francisco basket factory, 1925. Courtesy of Thomas W. Chinn, San Francisco, California.

17. Chinese woman with some of her children and neighbors in front of her grocery store in Nebraska. Courtesy of Thomas W. Chinn, San Francisco, California.

18. First Chinese pastor of the Chinese Presbyterian Church of San Francisco with his family. Courtesy of Thomas W. Chinn, San Francisco, California.

19. Second-floor office of the Chinatown Telephone Exchange, 1902. By Gabriel Moulin Studios. Courtesy of Ling-Gee Tom and Thomas W. Chinn, San Francisco, California.

20. Navajo women weaving blankets, ca. 1885. By Christian Barthelmess. Courtesy of the Museum of New Mexico, Santa Fe, New Mexico.

21. Apache woman, Na-tu-ende, ca. 1883. By Ben Wittick. Courtesy of the Museum of New Mexico, Santa Fe, New Mexico.

22. Pawnee Indian Wind Lodge, ca. 1868-1870. By William H. Jackson. Courtesy of the Museum of New Mexico, Santa Fe, New Mexico.

23. Indian children on the prairies, ca. 1912. Courtesy of Milton T. Theall, Weston, Massachusetts.

24. Maria Luna, ca. 1860. Bergere Collection, #21639. Courtesy of New Mexico State Records Center and Archives, Santa Fe, New Mexico.

25. Manuelita Lucero and husband, Jose Pablo Gallejos, ca. 1870, home in Abiquiu. SRC Misc. Collection, #24626. Courtesy of New Mexico State Records Center and Archives, Santa Fe, New Mexico.

26. Unidentified Hispanic woman at doorway. Sylvia Loomis Collection, #21951. Courtesy of New Mexico State Records Center and Archives, Santa Fe, New Mexico.

27. La Conquistadora Procession, Santa Fe. Sylvia Loomis Collection, #21987. Courtesy of New Mexico State Records Center and Archives, Santa Fe, New Mexico.

28. "The Country School," 1871, Winslow Homer, oil on canvas. Courtesy of the Saint Louis Art Museum, St. Louis, Missouri.

29. A university extension class in sewing, Brigham City, Utah. Courtesy of Special Collections and Archives, Utah State University, Logan, Utah.

30. Teaching contract from Trenton, Utah. Charles G. Wood Collection. Courtesy of Special Collections and Archives, Utah State University, Logan, Utah.

31. Mrs. C. I. Goff, teacher, in Midvale, Utah, one-room schoolhouse. S. George Ellsworth Collection. Courtesy of Special Collections and Archives, Utah State University, Logan, Utah.

32. Teacher's wage calculated by daily attendance. Courtesy of Special Collections and Archives, Utah State University, Logan, Utah.

33. District schoolbody, Montpelier, Idaho, 1890s. Courtesy of Special Collections and Archives, Utah State University, Logan, Utah.

34. Dominican Sister with pupil, St. Regina Academy, Madison, Wisconsin, ca. 1898. Courtesy of Archives of the Dominican Sisters of Sinsinawa, Sinsinawa, Wisconsin.

35. Mother Katharine Drexel. Courtesy of Archives of the Sisters of the Blessed Sacrament, Bensalem, Pennsylvania.

36. University of North Dakota, Grand Forks, North Dakota, 1904. "A View in the Armory." By George Blackburn. Courtesy of State

Archives and Historical Research Library, North Dakota Heritage Center, Bismarck, North Dakota.

37. Alice Eastwood, botanist. From *American West*, v. 27, January/ February, 1980.

38. Nurse assists at hospital in Brigham City, December 2, 1914. Courtesy of Special Collections and Archives, Utah State University, Logan, Utah.

39. Birdie McCarty, Prisoner #211, Photo #1081. Courtesy of the Kansas State Historical Society, Topeka, Kansas.

40. Salt Lake City prostitute posing for stereoscopics photo, ca. 1900–1906. Courtesy of Special Collections and Archives, Utah State University, Logan, Utah.

41. Unidentified prostitute. Courtesy of Boot Hill Museum, Dodge City, Kansas.

42. Dancing girl, Virginia City, Nevada. Courtesy of the Montana Historical Society, Helena, Montana.

43. Unidentified prostitutes. Courtesy of Boot Hill Museum, Dodge City, Kansas.

44. Montana State Prison wall construction, 1893. Courtesy of Montana Historical Society, Helena, Montana.

45. Lydia Howland, Prisoner #179, Photo #1050. Courtesy of Kansas State Historical Society, Topeka, Kansas.

46. Mary Bryant, Prisoner #230, Photo #1098. Courtesy of Kansas State Historical Society, Topeka, Kansas.

47. Goldie Jefferson, Prisoner #176, Photo #1049. Courtesy of Kansas State Historical Society, Topeka, Kansas.

48. Military wives with their husbands and children at Fort Davis, late 1880s. Courtesy of National Park Service: Fort Davis National Historic Site, Texas.

49. Sisters Eliason in front of their store, Logan, Utah, ca. 1905. Courtesy of Special Collections and Archives, Utah State University, Logan, Utah.

50. Woman doing needlework in Logan Canyon, Utah. Courtesy of Special Collections and Archives, Utah State University, Logan, Utah.

51. Women camping with children in a Utah canyon. Courtesy of Special Collections and Archives, Utah State University, Logan, Utah.

52. Women's baseball team from Cache Valley, Utah. Courtesy of Special Collections and Archives, Utah State University, Logan, Utah.

53. Woman at target practice. Smith Family Collection. Courtesy of Special Collections and Archives, Utah State University, Logan, Utah.

54. Hispanic child, New Mexico, ca. 1890. Courtesy of the Museum of New Mexico, Santa Fe, New Mexico.

55. Alice Butcher on the T. J. Butcher place on Middle Loup, West Union, Nebraska. By S. D. Butcher. Solomon D. Butcher Collection. Courtesy of Nebraska State Historical Society, Lincoln, Nebraska.

56. Genevra (Gene) Fornell at Lerroy, spring 1913. Courtesy of Montana Historical Society, Helena, Montana.

57. Wedding picture of Mr. and Mrs. James Sullivan, ca. 1870. By E. H. Train. Courtesy of the Montana Historical Society, Helena.

58. Unidentified Native American woman with baby. By Keystone View Co. Courtesy of the Museum of New Mexico, Santa Fe, New Mexico.

59. One method of Apache infant burial: cradleboard hanging from tree. Courtesy of Smithsonian Institution, National Anthropological Archives, Washington, D.C.

60. Charlotte T. Theall on snowshoes. Courtesy of Milton T. Theall, Weston, Massachusetts.

About the Authors

*A*nne M. Butler is coeditor of the *Western Historical Quarterly* and professor of history at Utah State University. She is the author of *Daughters of Joy, Sisters of Misery: Prostitutes in the American West, 1865–1890,* and has published extensively in western history on the subjects of social history and women's history.

*O*na Siporin has worked for fifteen years as a writer and storyteller in the artists-in-the-schools programs. She has been a guest narrator at the Bay Area Storytelling Festival, and is a regular resource artist at Sundance Institute. She is the author of Stories to Gather All Those Lost.